Cosmology

Bryan Milner

Series editor
Fred Webber

CAMBRIDGE
UNIVERSITY PRESS

Published by the Press Syndicate of the University of Cambridge
The Pitt Building, Trumpington Street, Cambridge CB2 1RP
40 West 20th Street, New York, NY 10011-4211, USA
10 Stamford Road, Oakleigh, Melbourne 3166, Australia

First published 1995

Printed in Great Britain at the University Press, Cambridge

A catalogue record for this book is available from the British Library

ISBN 0 521 42162 4 paperback

Designed and produced by Gecko Ltd, Bicester, Oxon

This book is one of a series produced to support
individual modules within the Cambridge Modular
Sciences scheme. Teachers should note that written
examinations will be set on the content of each module as
defined in the syllabus. This book is the author's
interpretation of the module.

Front cover photograph: Optical image of the Orion Nebula; Royal
Observatory, Edinburgh/AATB/Science Photo Library

Contents

Acknowledgements

4*tr*, 6*tr*, Dr Jeremy Burgess/Science Photo Library;
10*tr*, 37*tl*, Rev. Ronald Royer/Science Photo
Library; 13*bl*, Space Telescope Science
Institute/NASA/Science Photo Library; 21*b*, Fred
Espenak/Science Photo Library; 23, 39,
NOAO/Science Photo Library; 29, Department of
Physics, Imperial College/Science Photo Library;
31, Royal Observatory, Edinburgh/Science Photo
Library; 32*bl*, Tony Craddock/Science Photo
Library; 32*tr*, NASA/Science Photo Library;
38, Lick Observatory OP, University of California/
Science Photo Library; 40*cr*, Prof. Jocelyn Bell-
Burnell/The Open University; 40*br*, University of
Cambridge, Cavendish Laboratory, Madingley
Road, Cambridge (photographed by Edward
Leigh); 59, Science Photo Library

Prelude: Cosmology before Copernicus

By the end of this chapter you should be able to:

1 show familiarity with the astronomical observations which early models of the Universe were designed to explain;

2 understand how the most successful of these models explained the observations.

Cosmology is the study of the large-scale structure, the origins and the future of the Universe. It is a subject which makes very grand claims about an immense topic. Cosmologists today, for example, claim to know about objects which are billions of light-years away *(box P)* and to be able to describe, in detail, what happened during the first few seconds of the Universe nearly 20 billion (i.e. 2×10^{10}) years ago. [Note. Here, as elsewhere in this book, 'billion' is used in its now widely adopted American sense of one thousand million (10^9).]

In cosmology, as in other sciences, our present understanding has developed from earlier ideas.

Box P Light-years

Our normal units of distance – for example, metres and kilometres – are rather small compared to the enormous distances to stars and galaxies.

Astronomers often state the distance to a star or galaxy in terms of how long it takes light to travel from that star or galaxy to Earth, i.e. in **light-years**.

Light travels through space at $3.00 \times 10^8\,\mathrm{m\,s^{-1}}$ and a year is 3.15×10^7 seconds, so that a light-year is approximately $10^{16}\,$m.

Other units of distance used by astronomers are the **astronomical unit** (AU) and the **parsec** (pc). Details of these units can be found in *box 1B* and *box 2A* respectively.

SAQ P.1

Calculate the percentage error involved in using the figure of 10^{16} m for a light-year.

Sometimes these earlier ideas about the Universe turned out to be mistaken and had to be replaced by altogether different ideas; in other cases, earlier ideas are incorporated into our current cosmological theories.

The model of the Universe which cosmologists accept today really began with the model suggested by Copernicus in the sixteenth century and developed over the next 150 years or so by Kepler, Galileo and Newton. The Copernican model of the Universe, however, itself developed from earlier attempts to explain the patterns which can be observed in the apparent movements of the Sun, the Moon and the stars across the sky. To understand Copernicus' achievement, therefore, we need to know what these observable patterns are and how they were previously explained.

The basic patterns, which can be – and for thousands of years have been – observed with the naked eye, include the following:

■ The Sun rises in an easterly direction and moves westwards across the sky, rising higher in the sky during the first half of its journey and sinking back down to the horizon during the second half of its journey *(figure P.1)*.

■ There is a yearly pattern in the maximum angle above the horizon to which the Sun rises and in the length of time for which it is above the horizon. This pattern is related to the seasons: the Sun climbs highest in the sky and the daylight hours are longest during the summer.

■ The stars in the night sky are in fixed patterns – constellations – which rotate daily around a fixed point *(figure P.2a)*. At present, in the northern hemisphere, this point is close to Polaris, the Pole Star. There is also an annual pattern in the orientation of the constellations at midnight *(figure P.2b)*.

a

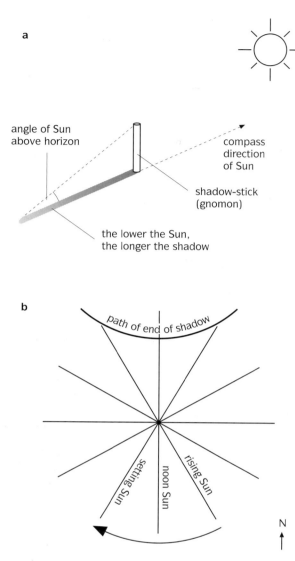

b

● **Figure P.1** Observing the movement of the Sun.

a A shadow-stick can be used to indicate the direction and elevation of the Sun.

b The pattern traced out by the shadow at mid-winter.

SAQ P.2

Use *figure P.1* to answer the following.

a How many hours are there between sunrise and sunset on the day shown on the diagram?

b Draw a similar diagram to show what happens at an equinox (one of the two days each year when there are exactly twelve hours between sunrise and sunset everywhere on Earth).

a

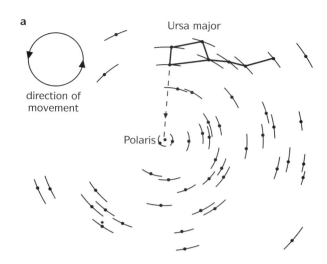

b midnight 1st January

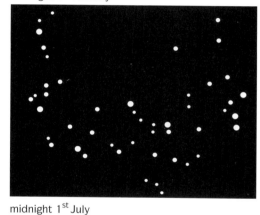

midnight 1st July

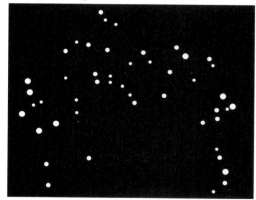

● **Figure P.2** Stars in a spin.

a The stars appear to rotate around the **celestial pole**, a point close to Polaris (the Pole Star), at very nearly 15° per hour. The constellation Ursa major (The Great Bear) is also called The Plough (in Britain), The Big Dipper (in the USA) and Le Casserole (in France).

b The positions of the stars at the same time of night also change during the year. [Note. The sizes of the stars on the diagram indicate how bright they are.]

SAQ P.3

Use *figure P.2b* to answer the following.

a By how many degrees, when viewed from the same point on Earth, have the constellations rotated around the celestial pole between midnight on 1 July, and midnight on 1 January?

b By how many degrees would the constellations appear to have rotated around the celestial pole between midnight on two successive nights?

Some people thousands of years ago, just like some people today, were not content with simply finding patterns in their observations: they wanted to be able to explain these patterns. To do this, they had to invent a *model* of what the Universe is like. In other words, they had to develop a cosmology. Various ancient civilisations developed cosmo-logical *stories* to explain their observations but the first *scientific* cosmologies we know about – that is, cosmologies which gave rise to definite predictions which could then be tested against further observa-tions – were developed by the ancient Greeks. One of these cosmologies – that of Ptolemy who lived in the second century AD – dominated European thought for the following 1400 years.

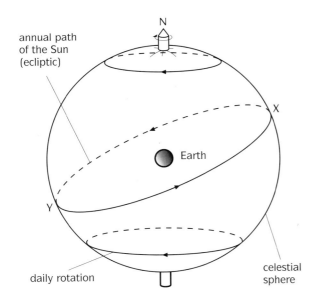

● **Figure P.3** The two-sphere model of the Universe. The spherical Earth is surrounded by a crystalline sphere which supports the stars. The Sun moves round this celestial sphere, taking one year to make a complete circuit.

Ptolemy's cosmology, like any other scientific model, explained observed patterns in terms of other ideas which were believed, at the time, to be true. For Ptolemy this included the following ideas:

■ the Earth itself is stationary;
■ things fall to the Earth unless supported;
■ unlike the imperfect Earth, where things change and decay, the heavens are perfect, unchanging and incorruptible;
■ the perfect three-dimensional shape is a sphere.

Applying these ideas to the patterns of movement of the Sun and the stars resulted in the two-sphere model of the Universe *(figure P.3)*.

SAQ P.4

Use *figure P.3* to answer the following.

a Draw a diagram to show why the Sun never sets at the Earth's north pole when the Sun is at position X of its annual path (ecliptic).

b What would you expect to happen at the Earth's north pole when the Sun is at position Y on its ecliptic? Explain your answer.

The ancient Greeks were aware, however, that they also had to account for the movements of the Moon and the five 'wandering stars' (planets) which slowly move against the background of the constellations *(figure P.4a)*.

To account for these movements, the two-sphere model was extended into a set of nesting crys-talline spheres: one sphere to carry the fixed stars, one sphere to carry the Sun, one sphere to carry the Moon and one sphere to carry each of the five known planets. The movements of these bodies across the sky were explained by their spheres rotating at different speeds and around slightly different axes *(figure P.5)*.

Unfortunately, the movements of the planets are not so straightforward as the movements of the Sun, the Moon and the constellations. The rate at which a planet moves through the constellations varies and it sometimes even moves in the opposite direction for a few weeks *(figure P.4b)*.

To explain this **retrograde motion**, the nesting-spheres model of the Universe had to be modified further: as a planet is carried by its crystalline

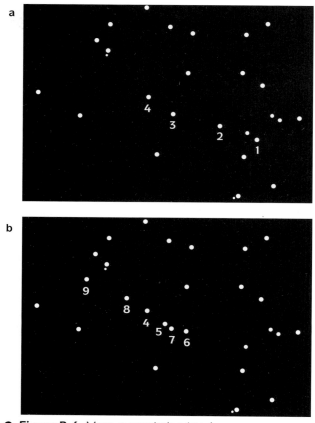

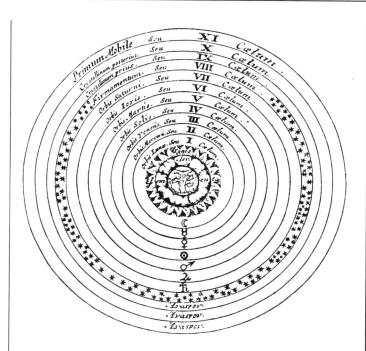

● *Figure P.4* Mars: a wandering 'star'.
The position of Mars is shown at monthly intervals.
[Note. The other planets move in a similar way, but at different speeds.]

a Mars normally moves in the same direction across the background of the constellations.

b Occasionally, however, Mars moves in the opposite direction for a while. This is called retrograde motion.

● *Figure P.5* Ptolemy's Earth-centred (geocentric) model of the Universe.

The planets which take longest to make a complete journey through the constellations are placed furthest from Earth. (*On average*, Mercury and Venus, as seen from Earth, take one year to make a complete journey through the constellations, so the relative positions of Mercury, Venus and the Sun on the Ptolemaic model are arbitrary.)

sphere at a steady speed around its main circular path (the **deferent**), it also moves around a smaller circle (an **epicycle**). When a planet is on the part of the epicycle closest to the Earth, its westward motion on the epicycle itself is greater than its eastward motion on the deferent so it moves through the constellations in the opposite direction to normal *(figure P.6)*.

SAQ P.5

Make a copy of the motion of Mercury around the Earth resulting from its epicycle *(figure P.6b)*.

Mark on your diagram the sections where Mercury's motion is retrograde.

In order to explain their increasingly accurate observations, Ptolemy and the later astronomers who used his system had to make more – and more complicated – modifications to the basic model. They had, for example, to introduce:

■ minor epicycles which rotated in the opposite direction to the deferent;

■ eccentrics, i.e. deferents which did not have the Earth as their centres;

■ equants, i.e. deferents with a non-uniform speed of rotation.

Though these modifications *worked* in the sense that they enabled astronomers to make increasingly accurate predictions of planetary movements, they made the theory less and less convincing as a model of the way in which the planets actually move. It was because he could no longer *believe* the Ptolemaic model that Copernicus proposed his revolutionary new model.

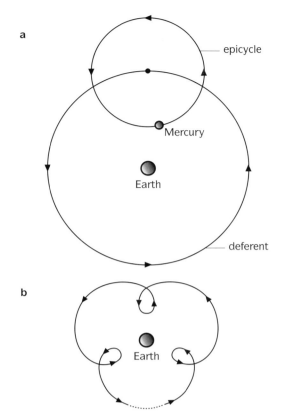

SUMMARY

■ Any model of the Universe needs to explain these familiar astronomical observations:
- the daily and annual patterns
  - in the apparent movement of the Sun across the day-time sky
  - in the apparent movement of the constellations across the night sky;
- the movement of the p anets against the background of the constellations, including their occasional retrograde moticn.

■ The Ptolemaic model of the Universe explained these observations in terms of:
- a geocentric system of rotating spheres carrying the Sun, the stars and the planets;
- complex adjustments, e.g. epicycles, to make the model fit the observed movements more exactly.

● *Figure P.6* Using an epicycle to explain the retrograde motion of Mercury.

a Mercury moves round its epicycle about three times, each time its centre moves around the deferent once.

b This means that Mercury retrogresses three times during each complete journey through the constellations.

Chapter one

The Copernican revolution

By the end of this chapter you should be able to:

1 describe how the work of Copernicus, Kepler and Galileo contributed to our understanding of the Universe;

2 use Newton's laws of motion, together with his theory of universal gravitation, to explain the orbits of the planets around the Sun;

3 give examples of how Newton's theory is supported by the predictions it made about the solar system.

Although it became increasingly complicated, the Ptolemaic model of the Universe accurately predicted the positions of the planets in the night sky so that astronomers – and astrologers who believed that planetary positions significantly affected human affairs – continued to use it. It was only towards the end of the seventeenth century that an alternative model, originally published by the Polish astronomer Copernicus in 1543, and developed during the following century by Kepler, Galileo and Newton, became widely accepted.

Copernicus

Nicolai Copernicus found the complexities of the Ptolemaic model, and the fact that it could often be modified in several different ways to make it match the same observations, altogether unsatisfactory. The model was, in his own words, 'neither sufficiently absolute nor sufficiently pleasing to the mind'. What Copernicus sought was 'a more reasonable arrangement of circles … in which everything would move uniformly about its proper centre'. To achieve this aim, Copernicus revived a model of the Universe with the Sun at its centre (a **heliocentric** model), first suggested by Aristarchus in the third century AD. He showed that this model provided a simpler, more believable, explanation for the observed movements of the Sun, the Moon and the planets than Ptolemy's Earth-centred

(**geocentric**) model. The retrograde motions of the planets could, for example, be readily explained without the need for epicycles (*figure 1.1*).

SAQ 1.1
Use *figure 1.1b* to explain why Mars is at its brightest during its periods of apparently retrograde motion.

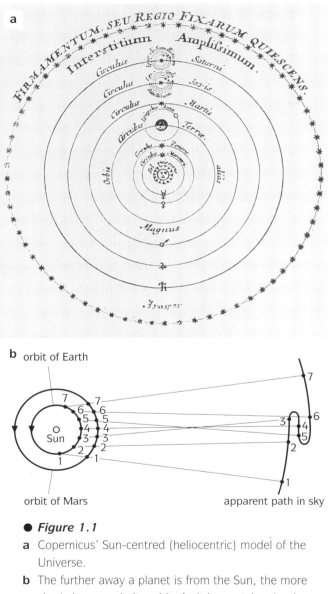

● *Figure 1.1*

a Copernicus' Sun-centred (heliocentric) model of the Universe.

b The further away a planet is from the Sun, the more slowly it moves in its orbit. As it is overtaken by the Earth, Mars appears to move the opposite way through the constellations.

Box 1A Parallax

Astronomers measure the relative positions of stars, planets, etc. in terms of the angles between the directions in which we see them. For precise measurement, each degree is divided into 60 minutes, and each minute into 60 seconds. In order to distinguish them from units of time, these small angles are referred to as minutes and seconds of **arc**, or as **arc-minutes** and **arc-seconds**.

Supporters of the Ptolemaic theory correctly argued that, if the Earth moves round the Sun, the angle between two stars on the stellar sphere should vary.

This variation in the angle between stars due to a change in the position from which they are observed is called **parallax**.

Astronomers now believe stars to be at different distances from Earth. The greater the difference in the distance of stars from Earth, the greater the parallax between them.

SAQ 1.2

Measure the parallax between the two stars on *figure 1.2*.

SAQ 1.3

Draw a diagram with the stars the same distance from each other but five times further away from the Sun. Measure the parallax again.

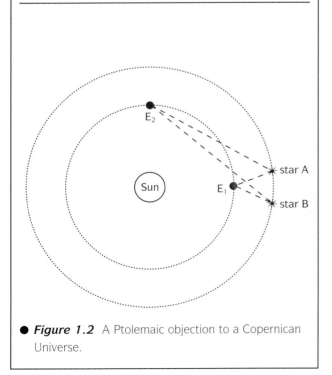

● **Figure 1.2** A Ptolemaic objection to a Copernican Universe.

Like many revolutionary ideas, Copernicus' theory met with a rather hostile reception when it was first published. There were several very good reasons for this.

First, the fact that a stone falls vertically to the ground when it is dropped, meant, for most scientists at that time, that the Earth could not itself be moving. Since Galileo and Newton had not yet revolutionised people's ideas about movement, this point of view was perfectly understandable.

Secondly, if the Earth really was moving around the Sun, the positions of the stars should change in relation to each other, i.e. there should be parallax between the stars *(box 1A)*. The famous Danish astronomer, Tycho Brahe (1546–1601), devoted his whole life to making much more accurate measurements of the positions of the stars and planets than ever before, partly to try to detect such parallax. Although he did his work before telescopes had been invented, Brahe was able to measure the directions of stars to better than half a minute of arc. Even so, he did not manage to detect any parallax and decided that Copernicus' heliocentric model must be wrong. Copernicus' position, however, like that of Aristarchus before him, was that the stars were much further away than was commonly supposed, so far away, in fact, that any parallax between them was too small to be detected: 'the dimensions of the world are so vast that though the distance from the Sun to the Earth appears very large ... yet compared with the dimensions of the sphere of fixed stars it is as nothing'. Copernicus was eventually proved right, but not until the nineteenth century when astronomers were able to measure the directions of stars to fractions of a second of arc.

A third, and at the time very serious, problem with Copernicus' model was that it could not be made to fit the observed positions of the planets exactly without introducing the very epicycles that the model was designed to get rid of. In fact, until it was improved by Kepler, Copernicus' model gave less accurate predictions of planetary positions than the Ptolemaic model which astronomers had been gradually improving for many centuries.

During the early part of the seventeenth century, however, the work of Kepler and Galileo, each in its own very distinctive way, helped to convince the majority of scientists that the Copernican model of the Universe was correct.

Kepler

Like the ancient Greeks, Johann Kepler believed that the Universe must have an underlying harmony and perfection. He was a convinced Copernican and devised a heliocentric model of the Universe in which the relative spacing of the six planets (the five naked-eye planets and the Earth itself) were matched, to an accuracy of better than 5%, by the spheres drawn inside and around the five regular solids: tetrahedron, cube, octahedron, dodecahedron and icosahedron *(figure 1.3)*.

Kepler became Brahe's assistant in the hope that more accurate data would show his version of the Copernican model to be correct. Kepler found, however, that he couldn't fit the observed positions of Mars on to a circular orbit at all, even using epicycles. Although the error was only about 8 minutes of arc, an error much smaller than Copernicus himself could have detected, Kepler knew that the measurements were reliable and, to his enormous credit, did not just ignore the discrepancy but struggled for years to find some way of making the theory match the facts.

Eventually Kepler realised that he could only make the planetary orbits fit the Copernican model if he dropped an assumption that both he and Copernicus had shared with the ancient Greeks: that the 'natural' path of a planet was a circle. If the orbit of each planet is an **ellipse** with the Sun at one of the foci – an idea which is now known as **Kepler's first law** – the Copernican model fits the observed data without the need for epicycles *(figure 1.4)*.

Jettisoning the perfectly shaped circular orbit in favour of an ellipse left Kepler with another

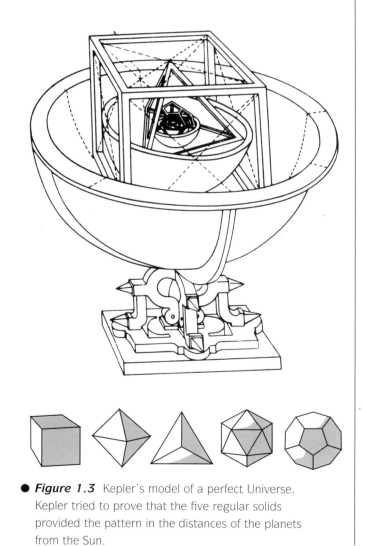

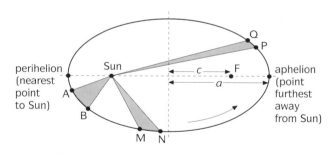

● *Figure 1.4* Kepler's first and second laws of planetary motion.

The orbits of the planets are ellipses with the Sun at one focus. F is the other focus. Distance *a* is called the semi-major axis.

The times taken to travel along AB, MN and PQ are equal. Since the shaded areas are also equal, the planet sweeps out the same area in any given interval of time. The **eccentricity** of the ellipse is given by *c*/*a*; for a circle *c* = 0 so the eccentricity is also zero.

[The diagram greatly exaggerates the small eccentricity of planetary orbits.]

● *Figure 1.3* Kepler's model of a perfect Universe. Kepler tried to prove that the five regular solids provided the pattern in the distances of the planets from the Sun.

problem: he could no longer assume that planets moved with a constant speed around those orbits. Once again, after a prodigious amount of work analysing the accurate data collected by Tycho Brahe and himself, Kepler found the relationship he was looking for: in any given period of time an imaginary line joining the Sun and a particular planet always sweeps out an equal area. This relationship is known as **Kepler's second law** *(figure 1.4)*.

Together, Kepler's first and second laws, published in 1609, enabled him to make complete and accurate predictions of the positions of the planets. However, Kepler was still not satisfied: so far he had a separate rule for each of the planets but – though he had been forced to give up not only his geometrical model, but also his idea of perfect, i.e. circular, motion – he still believed in a harmonious Universe. It took him a further ten years to find what he was looking for – the pattern we now know as **Kepler's third law**:

[orbital period]^2 $\propto$ [distance from Sun]^3

That is,

$$T^2 \propto d^3 \quad \text{and} \quad T^2 = kd^3$$

[Note. The 'distance from Sun' is strictly the semi-major axis.]

If the period of a planet is measured in years and its distance from the Sun is measured in astronomical units *(box 1B)*, then $k = 1$.

Box 1B The astronomical unit (AU)

When measuring distances within the solar system, a very convenient unit to use is the average distance between the Earth and the Sun.

This distance, which is very nearly 1.5×10^{11} m, is called the **astronomical unit** (AU).

SAQ 1.4
What would you expect to find if you drew a graph of T^2 against d^3 for the planets?

SAQ 1.5
The average distance of Mars from the Sun is 1.52 times the average distance of the Earth from the Sun. Calculate the orbital period of Mars.

SAQ 1.6
It takes Jupiter very nearly 12 years to make one complete orbit of the Sun. Calculate the approximate distance, in AU, of Jupiter from the Sun.

SAQ 1.7
The mean distance of the planet Saturn from the Sun is 9.54 AU. How far is this:

a in metres; **b** in terms of the speed of light?

In many ways, Kepler was a model scientist, passionate in his search for patterns yet careful in his measurements and prepared to modify even his most dearly held convictions in the face of conflicting evidence from those measurements. Though he was immensely successful in describing *how* the planets moved and hence explaining their apparent movement in relation to the constellations of fixed stars, Kepler did not manage to explain *why* the planets move in their elliptical paths. Providing this explanation was one of the great achievements of Newton during the latter half of the seventeenth century. By that time, most scientists had accepted the Copernican model of the Universe, partly because of Kepler's work but also because of the observations of Galileo through the recently invented telescope.

Galileo

In 1609, Galileo Galilei heard about how a Dutch lens grinder had used two lenses to make distant objects look larger and nearer. He tried the idea out for himself and then used it to look at the Moon, the planets and the stars. Galileo was a convinced Copernican and he was able to use what he saw to support his views. For example, his observation that there were mountains on the Moon helped to undermine the idea that the heavens were perfect, unchanging and altogether different from the Earth. His discovery that the Milky Way is made up of very many faint stars also supported Copernicus' idea about the great distances of the stars.

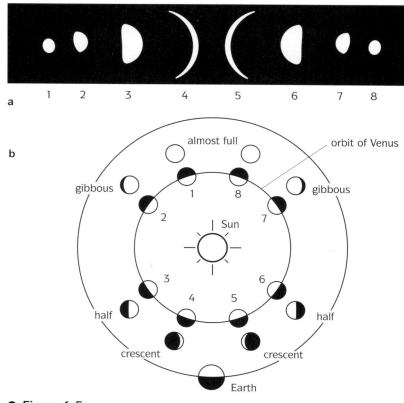

a

b

● *Figure 1.5*
a The phases of Venus.
b The Copernican model can readily explain these observations. [Note. For simplicity, the Earth is shown as being stationary. In fact, Venus orbits the Sun in approximately 60% of the time it takes the Earth to orbit the Sun.]

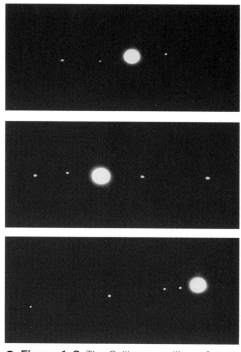

● *Figure 1.6* The Galilean satellites of Jupiter.
The photographs show what you can see if, like Galileo, you observe Jupiter through a telescope at intervals of a few days. The observations strongly suggest that there are four satellites ('moons') of Jupiter which orbit the planet at different rates.

More importantly, Galileo discovered through his telescope:

■ that Venus goes through a sequence of phases rather like the Moon, except that its crescent is part of a much larger circle than when it is nearly 'full' *(figure 1.5)*;

■ that Jupiter has four satellites ('moons'), which have since been called the Galilean satellites *(figure 1.6)*.

These observations strongly supported a Copernican model of the Universe.

SAQ 1.8 _____

Use *figure 1.5* to explain:

a why a crescent Venus is part of a much larger circle than a 'full' Venus;

b why Venus is also called the 'Evening Star' and the 'Morning Star'.

SAQ 1.9 _____

How could you show that Jupiter's satellites obey Kepler's third law?

Galileo also made important advances in our understanding of motion. Galileo's ideas were developed further by Newton who was then able to use them to help explain why the planets move in accordance to Kepler's laws.

Newton

Though Isaac Newton claimed that his contributions to science were possible only 'by standing on the shoulders of Giants ...', he was himself truly an intellectual giant. He made major advances, not only in the understanding of motion, including the motion of the planets, but also in many other branches of physics and mathematics.

Box 1C Newton's laws of motion

First law

A body continues in its state of rest or of uniform (i.e. unaccelerated) motion in a straight line unless it is acted on by a net (i.e. unbalanced) external force.

Second law

The acceleration produced in a body by an unbalanced force is in the direction of, and directly proportional to, the force and is inversely proportional to the mass of the body.

The second law is often expressed in the form

$$F = ma$$

where F is the net force in newtons, m the mass of the body in kg and a the resulting acceleration in $m\,s^{-2}$.

Third law

If a body A exerts a force on body B, then body B also exerts a force, of the same size and along the same line, on body A, but in the opposite direction.

Newton was also able to show that, for a body of mass m to move in a circular path of radius r with a speed of v, a force of $\frac{mv^2}{r}$ is needed, directed towards the centre of the circle (i.e. a **centripetal** force).

Building on the work of Galileo, Newton formulated the laws of motion as they apply to bodies on Earth *(box 1C)*. He then broke with the tradition that had begun with the ancient Greeks and applied these laws to the motion of heavenly bodies too. More specifically, he first proved that any spherical body which moves in accordance with Kepler's second law – sweeping out equal areas in equal times – must have a 'central' force acting on it. He also showed that, for a body moving in an elliptical orbit with the centre of force at one of the foci, this force must be inversely proportional to the square of the distances between the centres of the two bodies concerned. Newton then made the revolutionary suggestion that in the solar system this centrally directed force is, in fact, a **gravitational** force: just as the gravitational attraction of the Earth causes an object on Earth to fall to the ground when it is dropped, so the gravitational attraction of the Sun keeps a planet in its elliptical orbit.

Newton developed this idea by making two further assumptions about this gravitational force acting between any two bodies in the Universe:

firstly, that it is inversely proportional to the square of the distances between their centres (as he had already proved was required for motion in an ellipse); and, secondly, that it is directly proportional to their masses. In other words:

$$F \propto \frac{m_1 m_2}{d^2}$$

or

$$F = G\frac{m_1 m_2}{d^2}$$

This relationship is now known as the **law of universal gravitation** and the constant G as the **universal gravitational constant**.

Having boldly made all these assumptions, or **conjectures**, in developing his theory, Newton now needed to show that the theory gave the correct results when applied in practice, for example to the planets in the solar system.

Assuming that planetary orbits are circular (which they very nearly are), the gravitational force of the Sun on a planet has to supply the centripetal force needed to keep a planet in its orbit – that is,

$$G\frac{m_S m_P}{d^2} = \frac{m_P v^2}{d} \tag{1}$$

where m_S and m_P are the mass of the Sun and the planet, respectively; d is the Sun–planet distance; and v is the speed at which the planet moves round its orbit.

The period T of the planet, the time it takes to make one complete orbit of the Sun, is given by

$$T = \frac{2\pi d}{v} \tag{2}$$

Eliminating v by combining (1) and (2) gives

$$G\frac{m_S m_P}{d^2} = \frac{4\pi^2 m_P d}{T^2}$$

That is,

$$T^2 = \frac{4\pi^2 d^3}{G m_S}$$

Although this relationship shows that the theory of universal gravitation leads to Kepler's third law, it was not, by itself, enough to show that Newton's theory was correct. Newton also needed to show that his calculated values for the planetary periods T matched the observed values. Newton could not, in fact, calculate the planetary periods because neither the mass of the Sun nor the value of G was known. However, similar problems could be avoided when using the theory to calculate the orbital period of the Moon around the Earth *(box 1D)*.

When he first calculated the Moon's orbital period – in 1666, at the age of 24 – Newton was very disappointed that his figure was wrong by more than 16%. Sixteen years later, however, new measurements of the Earth's radius showed that the correct value was one-sixth larger than the previously accepted value. Using the new value, Newton's calculated figure for the Moon's period was only about 1% smaller than the observed figure. Now confident that he had firm evidence to support it, Newton published his theory of universal gravitation in 1686.

Further applications of Newton's theory to astronomy

If Newton had known the value of G, he would have been able to calculate:

- the mass of the Sun from the distance and period of any planet;
- the mass of any planet which has a satellite from the period and distance of that satellite.

However, it was over a century later when Henry Cavendish first succeeded in measuring G *(box 1E)* and so made it possible to use Newton's equations to calculate these masses.

SAQ 1.10 _____

Use the period of the Earth's orbit to calculate the mass of the Sun. (The value of G is given in *box 1E*.)

_____

The masses of planets which do not have satellites can be calculated by the small gravitational effects, or **perturbations**, they have on other planets *(box 1F)*. Observations of such perturbations in the orbit of the planet Uranus led to the discovery of the planet Neptune. Uranus itself was discovered by

---

Box 1D Calculating the Moon's period

Newton was not able to calculate the period T_M of the Moon directly from the expression

$$T_M^2 = \frac{4\pi^2 d^3}{Gm_E}$$

because, although he knew the Earth–Moon distance d, he did not know the value of the universal gravitational constant G or the mass of the Earth m_E.

He avoided this difficulty by applying his gravitational equation to falling bodies at the surface of the Earth:

$$F = mg = G\frac{mm_E}{r_E^2}$$

where g is the acceleration of falling bodies at the Earth's surface and r_E is the Earth's radius, both of which values Newton knew.

This means that

$$Gm_E = gr_E^2$$

and so

$$T_M^2 = \frac{4\pi^2 d^3}{gr_E^2}$$

Box 1E How Cavendish measured *G*

The major problem with measuring G is that if the bodies which are used to attract each other are of a measurable mass, the gravitational force between them is exceedingly small. Cavendish solved this problem using a very sensitive torsion balance *(figure 1.7)*.

When the large lead spheres were brought close to the smaller spheres, their gravitational attraction caused the suspension fibre to twist in proportion to the gravitational force.

The accepted figure for G is $6.67 \times 10^{-11} \, \text{N m}^2 \text{kg}^{-2}$.

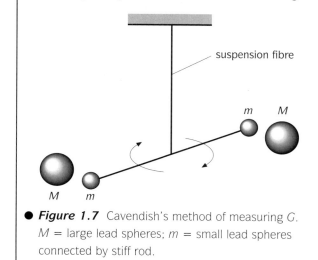

● *Figure 1.7* Cavendish's method of measuring G. M = large lead spheres; m = small lead spheres connected by stiff rod.

Box 1F Perturbations

As they move with different periods around their orbits, the distances between the various planets, and their mutual gravitational effects, are constantly changing. These changes produce wobbles, or **perturbations**, in the planets' orbits. Fortunately, these effects are quite small, otherwise they would have upset the calculations made by Kepler and Newton when developing their theories. Indeed, if the perturbations were very much bigger than they are, they would seriously affect the stability of the whole solar system. The perturbations are, however, large enough to measure and can then be used to calculate the masses of the bodies involved where these cannot be calculated from satellites. The collision between the comet Shoemaker-Levy 9 and the planet Jupiter in July 1994 *(figure 1.8)* was due to a massive perturbation. The comet was split into 21 pieces by huge gravitational forces as it passed close to Jupiter in 1992. The orbit of these pieces was also changed, resulting in the collision with Jupiter two years later.

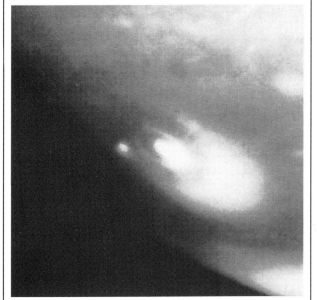

● *Figure 1.8* A perturbing catastrophe.
The site where a fragment of comet Shoemaker-Levy 9 hit Jupiter on July 18, 1994. The place of impact is seen as a bright spot at the centre surrounded by two ring-like features. The inner ring is 80% of the size of the Earth. This image was taken by the Hubble Space Telescope.

William Herschel in 1781 and, despite its very long period (84 years), enough measurements were made over the next few years to determine its orbit. By about 1830, however, it had become clear that Uranus was not moving in its calculated orbit, even when allowance was made for the perturbations caused by the other known planets. This meant that:

■ either there was something wrong with Newton's theory of gravitation;
■ or there was another, as yet undiscovered, planet causing perturbations.

In 1845, John Adams and Urbain Leverrier independently calculated exactly where another planet would have to be positioned to cause the observed perturbations. In 1846, the planet Neptune was discovered very close to this predicted position. What could have been a problem for Newton's theory proved instead to be the opportunity for a triumphant success.

During the early years of the twentieth century, astronomers discovered further perturbations in the orbits of both Uranus and Neptune. These suggested that their orbits were being affected by yet another planet and, after a long search, the planet Pluto was discovered in 1930. Many astronomers, however, consider Pluto's mass to be too small to explain the perturbations which led to its discovery.

SAQ 1.11
Use the information in *box 1G* to answer the following. In what ways is the planet Pluto different from other planets?

Problems for Newton's theory

Newton's laws of motion and his theory of gravitation have been spectacularly successful not only in explaining the motion of the Moon and the planets and predicting the existence of hitherto unknown planets, but also when applied to moving objects on the Earth. But even as Leverrier was using the theory to predict the existence of Neptune, he was aware that it didn't quite fit the observed behaviour of the innermost planet, Mercury. (For further information about this problem, and how it was resolved by Einstein's general theory of relativity, see *box 6D*.)

Finally, Newton was well aware that his theory of universal gravitation had important implications for the structure of the whole Universe. Since all the evidence available at the time indicated that the stars were static, Newton needed to explain why the gravitational attraction between them did not cause the Universe to collapse. Newton realised that there was only one solution to this problem: in a static Universe, matter must be uniformly spread throughout an infinitely large space. As astronomers since the time of Newton extended and developed an essentially Copernican model of the Universe in the light of further thought and evidence, the idea of an infinite, static Universe was shown to be mistaken. These developments in cosmological theory are explored in chapters 2–5.

Box 1G The solar system

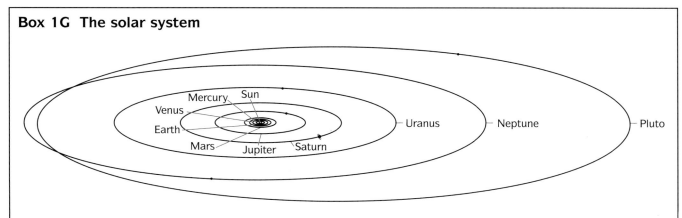

● *Figure 1.9* Planetary orbits. There is also a belt of small, rocky **asteroids** between Mars and Jupiter.

Planets

Table 1.1 summarises the facts and figures for the main planets in the solar system, while *figure 1.9* shows the planetary orbits and *figure 1.10* the relative sizes of the planets and the Sun.

In the table, the mass of each planet is compared with that of Earth, which is approximately 6×10^{24} kg.

The **ecliptic** is the plane of the Earth's orbit around the Sun.

Comets

Comets, which return at regular intervals, have very eccentric orbits around the Sun *(figure 1.11a)*. The first of these orbits was calculated by Edmond Halley, a friend of Newton, for the comet which now bears his name.

Comets are believed to be made from frozen water, methane and ammonia in which dust and fragments of rock are trapped. Typically, they are a few kilometres in diameter. When a comet is close to the Sun, a tail of vapour of the order of 1 AU long may be visible. This tail always points away from the Sun due to the pressure of the Sun's radiation *(figure 1.11b)*.

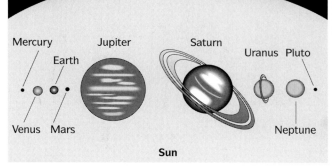

● *Figure 1.10* The relative sizes of the Sun and the planets.

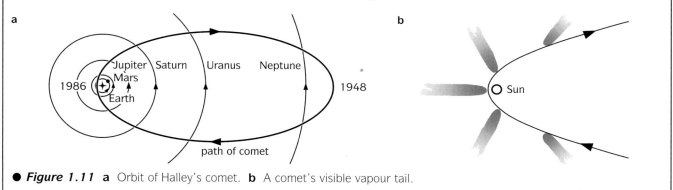

● *Figure 1.11* **a** Orbit of Halley's comet. **b** A comet's visible vapour tail.

Planet	Mean distance from Sun (AU)	Period (years)	Mass (Earth = 1)	Eccentricity	Inclination to ecliptic (degrees)	Number of known satellites
Mercury	0.39	0.24	0.06	0.21	7.0	0
Venus	0.72	0.62	0.81	0.01	3.4	0
Earth	1.00	1.00	1.00	0.02	0.0	1
Mars	1.52	1.88	0.11	0.09	1.9	2
Jupiter	5.20	11.9	318.0	0.05	1.3	16
Saturn	9.54	29.5	95.0	0.06	2.5	17
Uranus	19.2	84.0	14.5	0.05	0.8	15
Neptune	30.0	165.0	17.1	0.01	1.8	8
Pluto	39.5	249.0	0.002	0.25	17.1	1

● *Table 1.1* The planets of the solar system

Questions

1 In the Ptolemaic model of the solar system, Venus moves on an epicycle whose centre is on an Earth-centred deferent. The centre of the deferent is always directly between the Earth and the Sun *(figure 1.12)*.

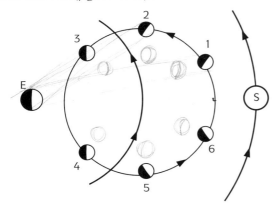

● *Figure 1.12* Venus in the Ptolemaic system.

a What does the Ptolemaic model predict about the phases of Venus?

b How does this prediction compare with what was actually observed by Galileo once the telescope had been invented?

2 In the eighteenth century, J. E. Bode and J. D. Titus generated a series of numbers as follows:

start with the series	0		3	6	12	24	48	96
add 4			4	7	10	...	...	...	...
divide by 10			0.4	0.7	...	...	...	...	...

a Complete the table of figures.

b Because Bode and Titus were astronomers, they were quite excited about the final series of numbers. Use the information in *table 1.1* to explain why. (Note. The planets beyond Saturn had not, at that time, been discovered.)

c Patterns in data are most useful to scientists if they not only fit existing observations but also predict new ones.

(i) What predictions could eighteenth-century astronomers make from the Bode–Titus series of numbers?

(ii) How successful did these predictions turn out to be?

SUMMARY

- Copernicus' heliocentric model of the Universe provided a more convincing explanation of the observed changes in the positions of the Sun, the planets and the stars than Ptolemy's long-established geocentric model.

- Kepler's laws of planetary motion are:
  1 planets move in elliptical orbits around the Sun;
  2 a particular planet sweeps out equal areas in equal times;
  3 the period T of a planet is related to its distance d from the Sun by the relationship $T^2 \propto d^3$.

  These laws helped to gain support for the Copernican model by increasing its accuracy and its simplicity.

- Further support for the Copernican model was gained by Galileo's discovery, through a telescope, of the phases of Venus and the satellites of Jupiter.

- The following three equations:
  - Newton's second law of motion: $F = ma$
  - Newton's theory of universal gravitation: $F = G\dfrac{m_1 m_2}{d^2}$
  - Newton's equation for circular motion: $F = \dfrac{mv^2}{r}$

  enabled Newton himself to explain Kepler's laws and to calculate the correct period for the Moon. They also enabled others to explain the regular return of comets and to predict the existence of the planet Neptune on the basis of perturbations in the orbit of Uranus.

Beyond the solar system

1 understand how the distances to stars can be measured;

2 know and explain how the brightness of stars is compared;

3 appreciate how astronomers established their ideas about the structure of the Universe beyond the solar system.

The Copernican model was primarily a model of the solar system; for Copernicus, as for Ptolemy, all the stars were simply placed on the outermost sphere of the Universe. One important difference, however, was that for Copernicus this outermost sphere of stars had to be very distant from the solar system, otherwise there would be detectable parallax between stars as the Earth moves round its orbit. This much greater distance of the stars implied that they did not, like the planets, simply reflect light from the Sun but actually emitted light like the Sun. In other words, the Sun is our local star and stars are distant 'suns'.

The distances of stars

During the seventeenth century, Galileo's discovery of many faint stars in the Milky Way and Newton's idea of an infinite Universe both indicated that stars were not all at the same distance from the solar system. Astronomers at that time, however, had no way of measuring the distances to stars. The best they could do was to assume that all stars were, in fact, equally bright and that differences in their **apparent** brightness (i.e. how

bright they looked) were entirely due to differences in their distances. The inverse square law was then used to compare distances: a star which was four times as bright as another would be only half as far away, a star nine times as bright only one-third as far away, and so on *(figure 2.1)*.

SAQ 2.1

Newton estimated that the Sun appeared from Earth to be a million million (10^{12}) times brighter than Sirius, the brightest star in the sky.

What would be Newton's estimate of the distance of Sirius from Earth?

By 1838, astronomical instruments were accurate enough for F. W. Bessel to measure the distance of the star 61 Cygni by its parallax, i.e. by the change in its direction relative to the directions of adjacent stars when measured from opposite sides of the Earth's orbit *(box 2A)*. The adjacent stars did not show any measurable parallax with each other and were assumed to be so far away that their directions remained virtually unchanged.

Using photographic techniques with the most accurate modern equipment, the smallest parallax which can be measured from the Earth's surface is

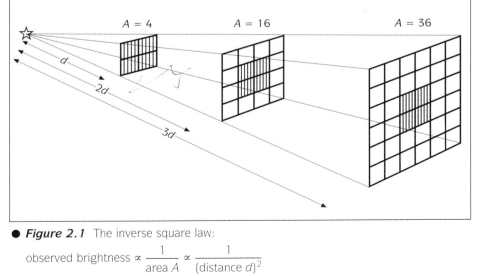

● *Figure 2.1* The inverse square law:

$$\text{observed brightness} \propto \frac{1}{\text{area } A} \propto \frac{1}{(\text{distance } d)^2}$$

Box 2A Using parallax to measure the distance of a star

Parallax p is defined as half of the angle through which a star's direction changes as the Earth moves from one extremity of its orbit to the other *(figure 2.2)*.

By measuring the direction of 61 Cygni with respect to more distant stars whose direction was assumed to remain the same, Bessel was able to measure its parallax.

The parallax of 61 Cygni

$$p = \frac{a + b}{2}$$

was just 0.3 seconds of arc.

Because the distances of the nearest stars are measured by their parallax, a star which has a parallax of 1 arc-second is said to be one par(allax) sec(ond) or **parsec** (pc) distant from Earth.

Since the further away a star is, the smaller its parallax,

$$\text{distance (pc)} = \frac{1}{\text{parallax (s)}}$$

61 Cygni is $\frac{1}{0.3}$ = 3.33 pc from Earth.

For a star at a distance of 1 parsec from Earth, the complete circumference of the circle of which a 1 AU arc is a part is given by 2π pc and by $60 \times 60 \times 360$ AU. That is,

$1 \text{pc} = 2 \times 10^5 \text{AU} = 3 \times 10^{16} \text{m}$ (which is 3.26 light-years)

61 Cygni is, therefore, about 11 light-years from Earth.

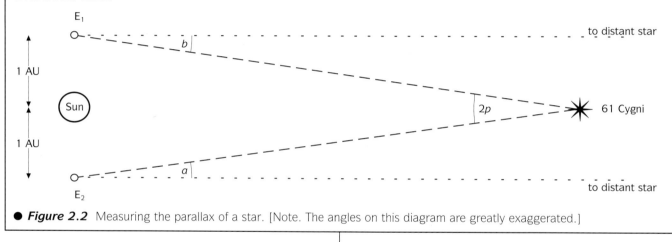

● *Figure 2.2* Measuring the parallax of a star. [Note. The angles on this diagram are greatly exaggerated.]

about 0.01 of a second of arc (a pin-head at a distance of ten miles!). This means that parallax can only be used to measure the distances of the 10 000 or so stars which are within 100 parsec of Earth. Fortunately, however, astronomers discovered how distances of certain stars could reliably be calculated from their brightness.

SAQ 2.2

The nearest star to Earth, other than the Sun, is Proxima Centauri which has a parallax of 0.76 seconds of arc. Calculate the distance of this star.

SAQ 2.3

How far away, in light-years, are the most distant stars whose parallax can be measured?

Stars were first classified according to their brightness more than two thousand years ago, by Hipparchus in ancient Greece. The brightest stars were classified as being **magnitude** 1; the dimmest stars which could be seen (with the naked eye – there were no telescopes in ancient Greece) were classified as being magnitude 6. Other stars were classified at intermediate magnitudes in accordance with how bright they looked.

During the nineteenth century, when it became possible to measure the intensity of the light reaching Earth from a star, scientists found that light from a magnitude 1 star was, in fact, about 100 times more intense than light from a star of magnitude 6. In other words, a *difference* of 5 magnitudes corresponds to a *ratio* of 100 in the measured intensity of light.

Since

$$2.5 \times 2.5 \times 2.5 \times 2.5 \times 2.5 = 2.5^5 = 100$$

a difference of 1 magnitude corresponds to a ratio of 2.5 in the measured intensity of light.

Being able to measure the amount of light received from stars also meant that the magnitude scale could be extended in both directions: the Sun has a magnitude of −26.7 and the dimmest star that can be detected on a long-exposure photograph using a very large telescope has a magnitude of about +25 *(figure 2.3a)*.

SAQ 2.4

How many times more intense is the light received on Earth:

a from a star of magnitude 1.7 than from a star of magnitude 4.7;

b from the Sun than from the brightest star, Sirius, magnitude −1.46?

How bright a star looks – its **apparent magnitude** – does not, however, tell us anything about how bright the star actually is. A star which looks very bright, for example, could be either a rather dim star which is not too far away from Earth or a very much brighter but more distant star. To be able to compare the actual brightness of stars, we must take into account how far away they are. Astronomers define the **absolute magnitude** of a star as the apparent magnitude it would have if it were 10 parsec from Earth. The absolute magnitudes of stars range from −10 to +15 *(figure 2.3b)*.

Using the inverse square law, it turns out that the apparent magnitude m, the absolute magnitude M and the distance d (in parsec) of a star are related by the expression

$$M = m - 5\log\left(\frac{d}{10}\right) \qquad \text{(Box 2B)}$$

Sirius, for example, has an apparent magnitude of −1.46 and is 2.65 parsec from Earth. The absolute magnitude of Sirius is given by the expression

$$
\begin{aligned}
M &= -1.46 - 5\log(0.265) \\
&= -1.46 - 5(-0.58) \\
&= -1.46 + 2.9 \\
&= +1.44
\end{aligned}
$$

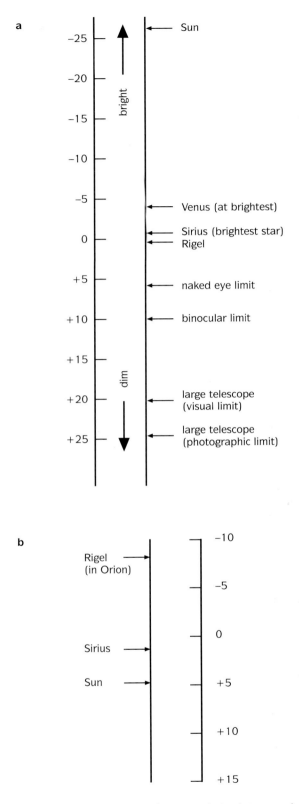

● *Figure 2.3* Apparent magnituces and absolute magnitudes of stars.

a Apparent magnitudes.

b Absolute magnitudes.

Box 2B Calculating the magnitudes of stars

The magnitudes of stars provide a way of comparing their brightness.

Since a difference in magnitude of 5 represents a brightness ratio of 100, the apparent magnitudes m_A and m_B of two stars from which the radiation reaching Earth has intensities I_A and I_B are given by the expression:

$$\frac{I_A}{I_B} = 100^{(m_B - m_A)/5}$$

[Note. A smaller magnitude implies a brighter star.]

That is,

$$\log\left(\frac{I_A}{I_B}\right) = \tfrac{2}{5}(m_B - m_A)$$

So, the difference in apparent magnitude is given by

$$m_A - m_B = -2.5\log\left(\frac{I_A}{I_B}\right)$$

The absolute magnitude M of a star is the apparent magnitude it would have if it were at a distance of 10 parsec. So

$$M - m = -2.5\log\left(\frac{I_{10}}{I}\right)$$

However, by the inverse square law,

$$\frac{I_{10}}{I} = \left(\frac{d}{10}\right)^2$$

So

$$M = m - 2.5\log\left(\frac{d}{10}\right)^2$$

$$= m - 5\log\left(\frac{d}{10}\right)$$

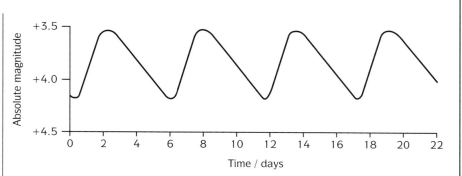

● *Figure 2.4* How the brightness of δ (delta) Cephei varies. This star has given its name to a whole group of variable stars called Cepheid variables.

SAQ 2.5

Arcturus is 11 parsec from Earth and has an apparent magnitude of −0.1. Calculate its absolute magnitude.

Henrietta Leavitt, in 1912, discovered how the brightness of stars called **Cepheid variables** could be used to calculate their distances. The brightness of these stars rises and falls in a very regular way *(figure 2.4)*, with periods ranging from a few hours to a few weeks. Fortunately for astronomers, some Cepheid variables are close enough for their distances to be measured by parallax. When she calculated the absolute magnitudes of these stars, Leavitt discovered a relationship between the absolute magnitude of a Cepheid variable and its period *(figure 2.5)*. Astronomers were then able to use this relationship to calculate the distances of Cepheid variables whose apparent magnitudes and periods could be measured but

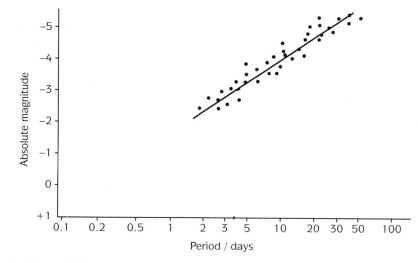

● *Figure 2.5* Absolute magnitude–period relationship for Cepheid variables. [Note. Walter Baade discovered, in 1952, that there are two distinct types of Cepheid variable. The graph is for what are known as Population I Cepheids.]

which were too far away to have any detectable parallax. Measuring the distances of Cepheid variables in this way played a crucial part in determining the scale, the structure and even the age of the Universe.

SAQ 2.6

Describe, in as much detail as you can, the pattern in the brightness of the star Delta Cephei shown in *figure 2.4*.

SAQ 2.7

Polaris is a Cepheid variable with a period of about 4 days. Its apparent magnitude varies around a figure of +2.0. Estimate the distance of Polaris from Earth.

Galaxies

The idea that stars were not just scattered randomly throughout space but were organised into large groups or **galaxies** was first suggested from observations of the Milky Way (*galaxias* is the Greek word for milk). The Milky Way is a faint, broad, continuous band of light which can only be seen on a clear, moonless night and when there is not too much light pollution from street lamps (*figure 2.6*). Galileo first noticed, via observations through a telescope, that the band of light was, in fact, a vast collection of very faint stars. Thomas Wright suggested, in 1750, that the continuous loop of the Milky Way could be explained if the

● *Figure 2.6* The Milky Way.

solar system were part of a collection of stars shaped like a convex lens. We see more stars when we look across the width of this galaxy than we do when looking across its thickness.

As this idea became accepted, astronomers naturally wanted to know how big the galaxy was and whereabouts in the galaxy the solar system was located. Detailed star counts in different sections of the Milky Way, made by William Herschel and his son John during the late eighteenth and early nineteenth centuries, gave the same results in all directions and suggested that the Sun must be quite close to the centre of the galaxy. Early in the twentieth century, however, Harlow Shapley used Cepheid variables to measure the distances of the globular clusters of stars which surround the galaxy (*figure 2.7*). His measurements indicated not only that the galaxy was approximately 100 000 light-years in diameter, but also that the Sun was rather closer to the edge of the galaxy than to its centre. The conflicting evidence from star counts was later explained in terms of dust within the galaxy which obscured the more distant stars. Studies of the clouds of hydrogen gas during the 1950s, using radiation in the 21-centimetre radio wave-band, indicated that the Milky Way has a spiral rather than a lens-like structure. The picture of the Milky Way which has gradually emerged is summarised in *figure 2.7*.

In 1755, Immanuel Kant had developed Wright's idea of the Milky Way as a galaxy of stars and

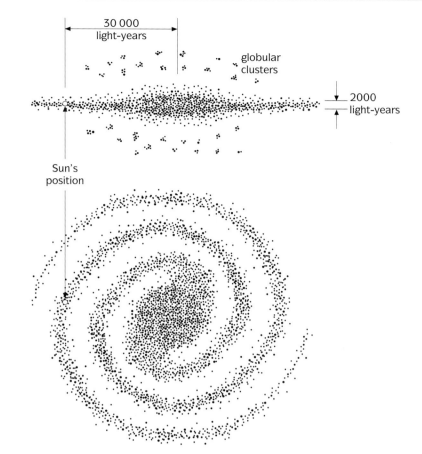

● *Figure 2.7* The size and structure of the Milky Way galaxy.

suggested that the luminous patches of light (nebulae) which can be seen in many parts of the night sky might also be galaxies of stars. Astronomers disagreed about this idea and it was not until 1924 that the existence of separate galaxies was confirmed when Edwin Hubble, using a 100-inch telescope, discovered Cepheid variables in the Andromeda nebula and in other spiral clusters of stars. These turned out to be much further away than the stars in our own galaxy. Hubble had shown that these spiral clusters were indeed separate galaxies of stars.

Hubble was able to use Cepheid variables to measure the distances of many local galaxies, i.e. galaxies up to about 2.5 million light-years away. When he calculated the absolute magnitudes of these galaxies, however, Hubble found that they were very similar: the difference in the magnitudes of the brightest and the dimmest galaxies was only about 2.5. Most galaxies are too far away to be able to pick out Cepheid variables but, by assuming that all these galaxies were of average brightness, Hubble was able to map out the Universe to a distance of 500 million light-years, a region which contains about 100 million galaxies (*box 2C*).

Hubble's measurements showed that although there are local variations in the Universe, so that the solar system, our own galaxy and

Box 2C More about galaxies

Galaxies may be spiral – like our own galaxy – or elliptical in shape *(figure 2.8)*. They are grouped into clusters with separate galaxies just a few galactic diameters apart.

Though they vary in size, galaxies typically contain around 100 billion stars. The fact that the stars which comprise galaxies are not observed to be falling towards the galactic centre suggests that they rotate around this centre. Evidence from 21-centimetre radio radiation within our own galaxy confirms this view. Stars which are nearer than the solar system to the galactic centre appear to move in the opposite direction to stars that are further away. This indicates that it is not the galaxy as a whole which rotates but that stars orbit the centre of mass of the galaxy in much the same way that planets orbit the Sun.

Using other galaxies as a fixed frame of reference, it is estimated that the Sun orbits the centre of mass of the Milky Way galaxy with a period of about 2.3×10^8 years.

The period of the Sun – or of any other star in the galaxy – is determined not by the total mass of the galaxy but by the mass of the galaxy which is within its orbit. The formula

$$T^2 = \frac{4\pi^2 d^3}{Gm}$$

can be used to calculate this mass, which can then itself be used to estimate the mass of the whole galaxy.

● *Figure 2.8* **a** Spiral galaxies.   **b** Elliptical galaxies.

our local group of galaxies all have their distinctive features, the Universe on a larger scale is very uniform. Just as the Earth's surface when seen from space no longer looks 'bumpy' but perfectly spherical, so the 'lumpiness' of the Universe is smoothed out when seen on a larger scale. The idea that the Universe is everywhere and in all directions essentially the same – i.e. that it is **isotropic** – is known as the **cosmological principle**.

Hubble's mapping of galaxies in effect completed the Copernican revolution. Far from being at the centre of the Universe as it was in the Ptolemaic model, the Earth is simply one of the planets of a star which is situated well away from the centre of one of the hundreds of millions of galaxies in the Universe. Hubble's detailed study of galaxies also led to what is often regarded as the most important astronomical discovery of the twentieth century, i.e. that the Universe is not static but expanding. The story of this discovery is included in chapter 5.

SAQ 2.8

Estimate the mass of the Milky Way galaxy (see *box 2C*).

SAQ 2.9

The difference between the apparent magnitude and the absolute magnitude of a Cepheid variable in the Andromeda galaxy is 29.

a   How far away is the galaxy?

b   How does the distance of the Andromeda galaxy compare with the diameter of the Milky Way?

SAQ 2.10

Summarise the overlapping methods used to measure the distances of stars and galaxies by making a table with the following headings:

Method used to measure distance

Distances measured (light-years)

SAQ 2.11

What is the biggest error Hubble would be likely to make in his estimates of the distances of distant galaxies by assuming they are all of average brightness?

SUMMARY

■ The observed brightness of stars is compared on an apparent magnitude scale on which the brightest stars visible to the naked eye are magnitude 1 and the dimmest stars magnitude 6.

■ The distances of the nearest stars can be found by measuring their parallax.

■ The absolute magnitude M of a star is related to its apparent magnitude m and its distance d (in parsec) by the expression:

$$M = m - 5 \log \frac{d}{10}$$

■ A relationship exists between the absolute magnitude and the period for Cepheid variables. This greatly extends the range over which the distances to stars can be measured.

■ Observations of the Milky Way suggest that it is a spiral galaxy of stars and that the Sun is well away from its centre.

■ Distance measurements indicate that the Milky Way is but one of many millions of galaxies, local clusters of which are uniformly distributed in all directions (the cosmological principle).

Question

1 The speed at which stars are moving towards or away from the Earth can be measured from the Doppler shift of their spectra. (See chapter 5 for an explanation of this.)

Figure 2.9 shows these speeds for stars in different parts of the galaxy, after making allowance for the speed of the galaxy as a whole.

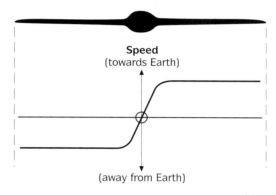

● *Figure 2.9* Speeds (relative to Earth) of stars in different parts of a galaxy.

Explain as fully as you can, what the data in *figure 2.9* indicates about the galaxy.

Chapter three

Reading the radiation from stars

By the end of this chapter you should be able to:

1 understand how the light, and the other electromagnetic radiation, which reaches Earth from space can be used:
  - to calculate the temperature of stars;
  - to identify the chemical elements from which stars are made;
  - to group stars into a small number of types;

2 appreciate why some types of electromagnetic radiation from stars can only be observed from above the Earth's atmosphere.

The only source of information astronomers have about stars is from the light – and the radiation from other parts of the electromagnetic spectrum – which reaches Earth. Astronomers have learned to use this radiation not only to measure the distances of stars and galaxies but also to measure the temperatures of stars and to find out what chemical elements they are made of. Information about the temperatures and composition of stars eventually helped astronomers to work out the different stages in the life-histories of stars.

The temperatures of stars

Astronomers can tell how hot the surface of a star is by the colour of the light it emits. To understand how they do this, think about what happens as you gradually increase the current through the filament of a light bulb. When the filament becomes hot enough it starts to emit light. At about 800 K (K = °C + 273), the filament emits a dull red glow, i.e. it has become red-hot. As its temperature rises further, not only does the filament emit more light but the colour of the light it emits also changes, first to orange and then to yellow. Eventually, if the filament can be made hot enough, it emits white light or even light which looks distinctly blue.

If you look carefully at stars, you will notice that they too may be any colour in the range from red, through yellow and white, to blue, so that the colour of a star gives a good indication of its surface temperature. Stars are often classified by their colours – and hence, in effect, by their temperatures – using a scale devised in Harvard at the beginning of the twentieth century (box 3A).

Box 3A Classifying stars by their colour

Since the beginning of the twentieth century, stars have been classified according to their **spectral type**, i.e. the colour of the light they emit. In effect, this is classifying stars by their temperatures. Table 3.1 summarises this classification.

The actual letters used for spectral type are a relic from a century or so ago when stellar spectra were classified into many more types and before the relationship between spectral type and temperature was recognised.

Spectral type	Colour	
O	blue	hottest
B	blue-white	
A	white	
F	yellow-white	
G	yellow	
K	yellow-orange	
M	red	coolest

● **Table 3.1** The classification of stars

SAQ 3.1

Sirius is a very bright white star. Betelgeuse and Arcturus are both red, but Arcturus is rather more orange than Betelgeuse. Rigel is a blue star.

Put these stars in order of their temperatures, starting with the hottest.

To understand why the colour of a hot body changes as its temperature changes, we need to split up the radiation it emits into a **spectrum** of its different wavelengths using a transparent prism or a diffraction grating (figure 3.1).

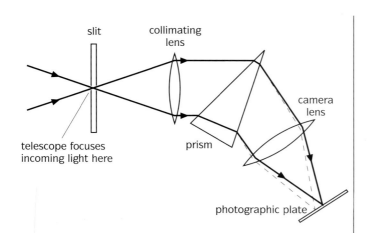

● *Figure 3.1* Splitting radiation into a spectrum.
The collimating lens produces a parallel beam of light.
Different wavelengths are deviated different amounts by
the prism and are brought to a focus at different points
on the photographic plate.
Lenses and prisms absorb light; a better **spectrometer**
can be made using mirrors and a diffraction grating.
The intensities of different wavelengths can also be
directly measured electronically.

Once radiation has been split into a spectrum, its
intensity at each wavelength can be measured. A hot
solid body emits radiation across a broad range of
wavelengths, with a peak intensity at one particular
wavelength. The higher the temperature of a body:

■ the shorter the wavelength at which peak intensity occurs; and

■ the greater the intensity at each wavelength, i.e.
the higher the overall rate at which a given area
of its surface radiates energy *(figure 3.2)*.

The radiation profile of a hot body depends not
only on its temperature, but also on the nature of
its surface. Surfaces which are good absorbers (and
therefore poor reflectors) of a particular wavelength of radiation are also good emitters of those
wavelengths. A perfectly black surface is one which
absorbs all the light radiation which falls on it. We
can extend this idea to include all other types of
electromagnetic radiation and imagine a perfectly
black body which absorbs all the radiation which
falls on it. Such a black body would also be a
perfect emitter of all wavelengths of electromagnetic radiation.

In 1893, using the best black body he could
make, Wilhelm Wien discovered the following
relationship between the temperature T and the
wavelength which has the maximum rate of energy
emission λ_{max}:

$$\lambda_{max} T = \text{constant}$$

(If T is in kelvin and λ_{max} in metres, the constant
equals $2.9 \times 10^{-3} \, \text{m K}$.)

This relationship is now known as **Wien's
displacement law.**

If λ_{max} for a body is measured, its temperature
can then be calculated. For example, if the filament
of an electric light bulb emits more energy at a
wavelength of 1×10^{-6} m than at any other wavelength, the temperature of the filament is given by

$$\lambda_{max} T = 2.9 \times 10^{-3} \, \text{m K}$$

That is,

$$T = \frac{2.9 \times 10^{-3}}{1 \times 10^{-6}} \, \text{K}$$

$$= 2900 \, \text{K}$$

This calculated temperature, which is called the
black-body temperature, will not be exactly right

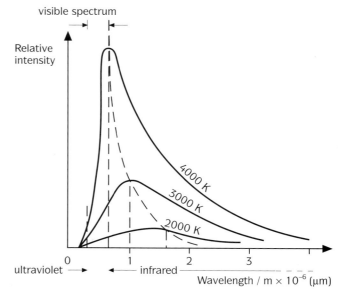

● *Figure 3.2* Radiation energy profiles at different
temperatures.
The broken lines show how the peak intensity, and the
wavelength at which this occurs, vary with temperature.
The overall intensity is represented by the area under
the graphs.

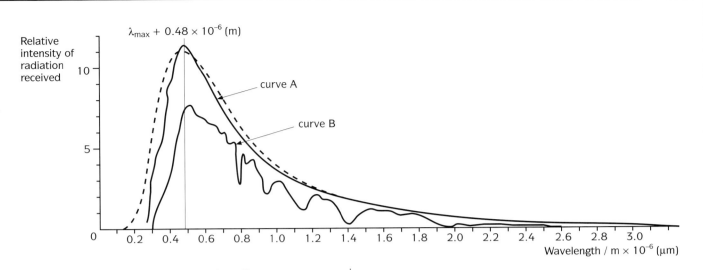

$\lambda_{\text{max}} + 0.48 \times 10^{-6}$ (m)

Relative intensity of radiation received

curve A

curve B

Wavelength / m × 10⁻⁶ (μm)

● *Figure 3.3* The Sun as a black-body radiator. The broken curve is for black-body radiation. Curve A is radiation from the Sun which reaches the Earth's atmosphere. Curve B is radiation from the Sun which reaches the Earth's surface.

because the filament is not a perfectly black body. The surface of a star is, however, believed to be very nearly a black body so that measuring λ_{max} gives a reliable measurement of its temperature (*figure 3.3*).

SAQ 3.2

Use the information from *figure 3.3* to calculate the temperature of the Sun's surface.

Early in the twentieth century, some interesting patterns were discovered by plotting, on a graph, the absolute magnitude of stars against their temperature. Such a graph is now called a **Hertzsprung–Russell diagram** (H–R diagram), after the two astronomers who separately discovered these patterns (*figure 3.4*).

Most of the stars on an H–R diagram fall on a band crossing the diagram diagonally from top left to bottom right. These are known as **main sequence** stars.

There is a cluster of relatively cool, red stars in the top right quarter of the H–R diagram whose absolute magnitudes indicate that they are very bright. Since a cool star radiates energy at a relatively low rate per unit area, these stars must be very large. Typically they have diameters 10–100 times greater than the Sun and are known as **red giants**.

Finally, there is a cluster of relatively hot, white stars in the bottom left quarter of the H–R diagram. The absolute magnitudes of these stars indicate that they are rather dim. Since a hot star radiates energy at a relatively high rate per unit area, these stars must be very small. Typically they are about the size of the Earth, i.e. about one-thirtieth the diameter of the Sun, and are known as **white dwarfs**.

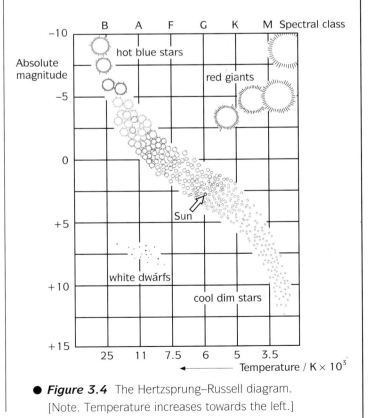

● *Figure 3.4* The Hertzsprung–Russell diagram. [Note. Temperature increases towards the left.]

27

Box 3B Using binary star systems to estimate stellar masses

About half of the stars we can see are members of multiple star systems in which two or more stars orbit each other. By carefully observing the orbits of the two stars in a binary system, astronomers can calculate their masses.

There are some binary star systems in which both stars are visible. The period of the orbit of either star around the other can then be measured *(figure 3.5a)*. Provided the distance of the stars from Earth is known, the distance between the stars can be calculated from their angular separation. Their combined mass can then be calculated from the following relation, derived by Newton from Kepler's third law (though not applied by him to binary stars):

$$m_1 + m_2 = k \frac{a^3}{T^2}$$

where $m_1 + m_2$ is the combined mass of the two stars, a is the distance between them, and T is the orbital period in years.

If m_1 and m_2 are in terms of the Sun's mass and a is in AU, then $k = 1$.

In actual fact, each of the two stars in a binary system orbits their common centre of mass which does not itself move against the background of stars *(figure 3.5b)*.

The relative masses of the stars are inversely proportional to their relative distances from this common centre of mass. The individual mass of each star can be calculated from their total mass and their relative masses.

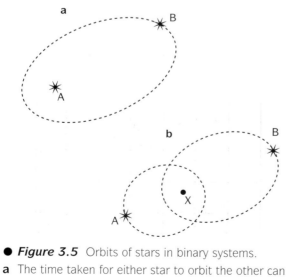

● *Figure 3.5* Orbits of stars in binary systems.
a The time taken for either star to orbit the other can be measured.
b In actual fact, both stars orbit their common centre of mass, X.

SAQ 3.3
Comment on the position of the Sun on the H–R diagram.

By estimating the masses of stars *(box 3B)*, astronomers discovered that there was a relationship between the mass of a main sequence star and its position on an H–R diagram. The hottest, brightest stars at the top left of the main sequence on an H–R diagram are the most massive (up to about 50 times the mass of the Sun). The coolest, dimmest stars at the bottom right of the diagram are the least massive (as little as 0.05 of the mass of the Sun).

The composition of stars

Oddly enough, we can find out which chemical elements stars are made of from the radiation we *don't* receive from them. To explain this, we need to understand what is happening to the atoms of a substance when they emit radiation.

An atom comprises a very small, massive nucleus surrounded by a much larger volume which is occupied by electrons. When an atom absorbs energy, one or more of these electrons may become excited, i.e. 'jump' to a higher energy level. If an excited electron then returns to its original energy level, energy is released as radiation. The wavelength of the radiation emitted by a particular electron depends on precisely the amount of energy it releases as it returns to its unexcited state. The larger the amount of energy released by an electron, the higher the frequency – and the shorter the wavelength – of the radiation it emits.

When atoms are very close together, as they are in a solid or in the dense matter of a star, there are so many different interacting forces that the electrons in atoms make energy jumps of all sizes within a certain range. This will produce radiation of all frequencies within a certain range, so a **continuous spectrum** is produced.

If atoms are well separated, however, as they are in a gas, the forces of interaction between them will be very small except when they are actually colliding. The electrons in each particular type of atom, therefore, have only a relatively small number of possible energy levels. Whenever an

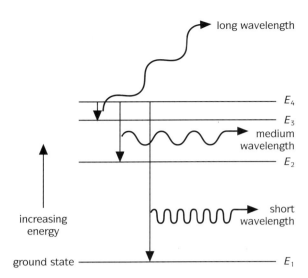

● *Figure 3.6* Electron jumps and radiant energy. When electrons 'jump' from a higher energy level to a lower one, radiation is emitted. The larger the energy jump, the shorter the wavelength of the radiation emitted.

electron releases energy by moving between a particular pair of these levels, exactly the same amount of energy is released and exactly the same wavelength of radiation is emitted *(figure 3.6)*.

In a gas, each type of atom emits its own distinctive wavelengths of radiation; when these are separated, using a prism or diffraction grating, the resulting **emission spectrum** consists of a set of narrow lines. Individual elements can be identified by the particular lines in their emission spectra, just as individual human beings can be identified by their particular fingerprints *(figure 3.7)*.

SAQ 3.4

Explain why a sodium vapour lamp, a mercury vapour lamp and a neon sign each produces its own distinctive colour of light.

The spectrum produced by the radiation from a star, however, is neither an emission spectrum consisting of bright lines nor a continuous spectrum. It is, in fact, a continuous spectrum with *dark* lines where certain wavelengths of radiation are missing. These lines were first discovered in the Sun's spectrum by Joseph von Fraunhofer, in 1814, and are now known as **Fraunhofer lines** *(figure 3.8a)*.

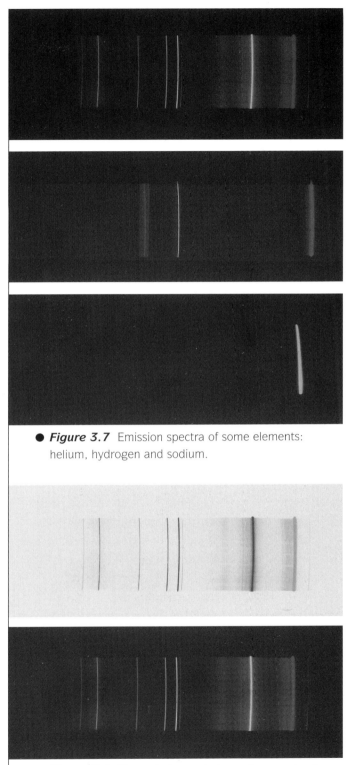

● *Figure 3.7* Emission spectra of some elements: helium, hydrogen and sodium.

● *Figure 3.8* The emission and absorption spectra for helium.
Dark lines in the absorption spectrum of any element exactly match the bright lines in its emission spectrum.
a Absorption spectrum.
b Emission spectrum.

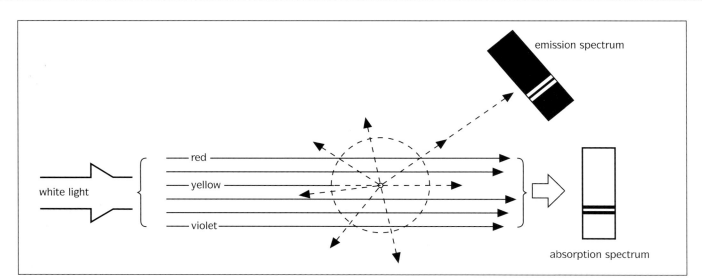

● *Figure 3.9* How an absorption spectrum is produced.
For simplicity, only the strong lines in the yellow region of the spectrum are shown. Yellow light
at these two wavelengths is absorbed by the sodium atoms and re-emitted in all directions.
The intensity of these wavelengths travelling in the original direction is, therefore, greatly reduced.

Fortunately, we can learn just as much from Fraunhofer lines as we can from an emission spectrum. Most of the radiation from a star is emitted from its very hot surface. The dark lines are produced because atoms in the somewhat cooler atmosphere of stars absorb exactly the same wavelengths of radiation that they emit. Of course, they continually re-emit this radiation, but they do so in all directions so that much less is emitted in the direction it was originally travelling *(figure 3.9)*.

The dark Fraunhofer lines are, therefore, the **absorption spectra** of the elements in the atmosphere of the Sun or stars and are at exactly the same wavelengths as the bright lines in the emission spectra of those elements *(figure 3.8b)*. By matching the lines in a star's absorption spectrum with the lines in the emission spectra of elements, astronomers can identify the chemical elements in the atmosphere of the star *(figure 3.10)*. Of the 92 naturally occurring elements, 67 have been detected in the Sun and one of these elements – helium – was first discovered there *(box 3D)*.

Finally, it is important to remember that radiation reaches Earth from space not only as light but also from across the whole electromagnetic spectrum. Astronomers have, since the late 1930s, discovered

a great deal about the Universe from their observations of these other types of radiation and by interpreting their spectra in just the same way as they had learned to interpret visible spectra *(box 3C)*.

SAQ 3.5

Explain what the spectra in *figure 3.10* indicate about the Sun's atmosphere.

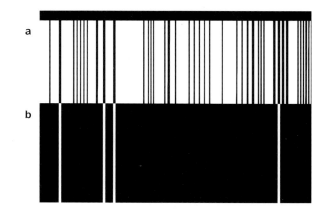

● *Figure 3.10* Detecting elements in the Sun.
a Dark lines in the (absorption) spectrum of sunlight.
b The emission spectrum for iron in the same range of wavelengths.

Box 3C Reading radiation from the electro-magnetic spectrum *(continued on page 32)*

Radiation from stars and galaxies reaches the Earth not only as light but also from other regions of the electromagnetic spectrum. Until the mid-twentieth century, however, astronomers concentrated entirely on visible radiation. One obvious reason for this is that they could detect this radiation with their own eyes, whereas other types of radiation have to be detected in some other way – for example through using special film or electronic devices.

It is important to realise that the Earth's atmosphere only allows radiation in two bands of wavelengths to pass through easily *(figure 3.11)*. One of these 'windows' corresponds quite closely to the range of visible wavelengths, though it also extends partly into the infrared and ultraviolet regions of the electromagnetic spectrum. The other band of radiation for which the atmosphere is transparent is radio waves with wavelengths between about 10 centimetres and 100 metres.

Earth-based telescopes

The atmosphere is not, however, perfectly transparent for light. This is partly due to absorption by molecules in the atmosphere and partly due to scattering, mainly by dust particles but also to some extent by molecules. This is why large – and expensive – **optical telescopes** are placed in observatories on high mountain sites *(figure 3.12)* in parts of the world which are as free as possible from atmospheric pollution and the light pollution which street lights in towns

and cities create. Observations in the near infrared region of the electromagnetic spectrum are also possible from such sites.

The existence of an atmospheric window for a band of radio waves explains why the first non-optical telescopes developed by astronomers were **radio telescopes** *(figure 3.13)*. The first observations of radio waves from astronomical bodies were made during the 1930s.

● *Figure 3.12* The 1.2 metre UK Schmidt optical telescope, on a remote mountain in New South Wales, Australia. This is used to photograph the southern sky. Each 0.33 m × 0.33 m photographic plate contains images of up to a million stars and galaxies. Galaxies up to 10^9 light-years away are recorded.

Key

☐ transparent

▨ partial absorption

■ opaque

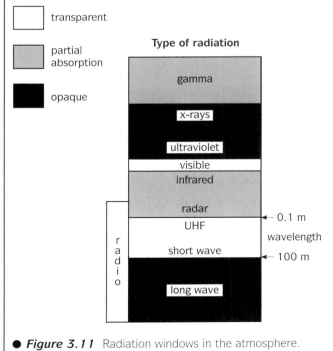

Type of radiation

gamma
x-rays
ultraviolet
visible
infrared
radar
UHF   ← 0.1 m
             wavelength
short wave   ← 100 m
long wave

radio

● *Figure 3.11* Radiation windows in the atmosphere.

On the 4200 m summit of Mauna Kea, in Hawaii, there are nine major telescopes: three for short radio wavelengths, and six for visible and infrared radiation.

Telescopes in space

To make observations at visible wavelengths which are entirely unaffected by the Earth's atmosphere requires using a spaceship or artificial satellite as the observation platform. Doing this is, of course, very expensive. The Hubble telescope, for example, which was put into orbit in April 1990, cost $1.2 billion. In December 1993 it cost a further $630 million to correct design faults which were only discovered once the telescope was in orbit *(figure 3.14)*.

Effective observation of radiation at other wavelengths requires putting the detection devices into orbit above the Earth's atmosphere. Examples of these include:

- the High Energy Astrophysical Observers (X-ray) (HEAO), 1977–79;
- the International Ultraviolet Explorer (IUE), 1978;
- the Infrared Astronomical Satellite (IRAS), 1983;
- the Cosmic Background Explorer Satellite (microwave) (COBE), 1989.

Some of the discoveries astronomers have made from observations in these regions of the electromagnetic spectrum are included at various places in this book.

● *Figure 3.14* The Hubble telescope.

Can we afford cosmology?

Because of the very high cost of putting satellites into orbit, astronomers have to fight hard to obtain the necessary funding. This has become increasingly difficult especially since satellites designed to find out, for example, about distant parts of the Universe – unlike communications satellites and weather satellites – have no obvious economic pay-off.

Indeed, funding for astronomical research of any kind, as for any other scientific research that is not directly targeted at enhancing the economy, is under increasing pressure. A good *standard of living*, including expensive items such as health care, a safe environment and national security, is obviously very important. However, *quality of life*, which includes not only the arts but also the quest for a better understanding of the Universe simply because of the desire to know, is considered by many people to be equally important. Getting the balance right, especially when the quality of many people's lives could be greatly increased by improving their standard of living, raises serious political and moral issues.

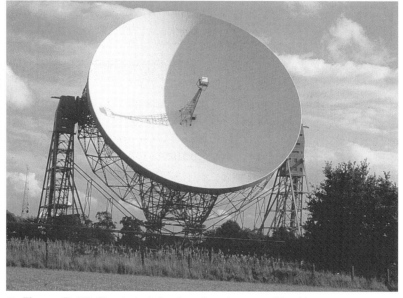

● *Figure 3.13* The Jodrell Bank radio telescope, Cheshire.

Box 3D Elements in the Sun

Table 3.2 shows how many atomic nuclei there are of each of the commonest elements for each 10^6 hydrogen nuclei (protons).

Number of atomic nuclei	Elements
1 000 000	hydrogen
60 000	helium
100–1000	oxygen, carbon
10–100	nitrogen, silicon, neon, magnesium, iron, sulphur
1–10	sodium, aluminium, argon, calcium, nickel

● **Table 3.2** The proportions of different elements in the Sun

How helium was discovered

In 1868, Norman Lockyer noticed in the Sun's spectrum a line that did not correspond to any known element. Lockyer had discovered a new element which he called helium after the Greek word for the Sun – *helios*. More than 20 years later, a gas which was released when heating uranium ore was found to produce the same lines in its emission spectrum. We now know that the alpha (α) radiation emitted by radioactive uranium atoms consists of particles which are, in fact, the nuclei of helium atoms. Though there is very little helium on Earth, helium is the second most common element in the Sun, in other stars, and in the Universe as a whole.

SUMMARY

■ The radiation emitted by stars can be split up into spectra so that we can examine the different wavelengths of radiation they contain.

■ The temperature of a star can be measured by identifying the wavelength at which most energy is emitted and comparing this with what we know about the energy emitted by a black body at different temperatures.

■ The chemical elements present in stars can be identified by comparing the dark lines in stellar spectra with the absorption spectra of the separate elements.

■ Plotting the absolute magnitudes of stars against their temperatures on a Hertzsprung–Russell diagram indicates that there are three types of star:
  ● main sequence stars,
  ● red giants and
  ● white dwarfs.

■ The Earth's atmosphere is transparent only to electromagnetic radiation in the regions of light and shorter wavelength radio waves. Electromagnetic radiation from stars in other regions of the electromagnetic spectrum can be observed only from above the Earth's atmosphere.

Question

1 *Figure 3.15* shows how the movement of two adjacent stars, towards or away from Earth, varies with time. (These speeds can be measured from the Doppler shift of their spectra as explained in chapter 5.)

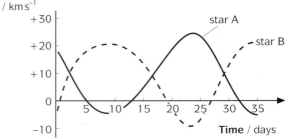

● **Figure 3.15** Speeds (relative to Earth) of two adjacent stars.

Explain, in as much detail as you can, what *figure 3.15* suggests about the two stars.

The life-histories of stars

1 understand how stars are formed;

2 demonstrate awareness of the thermonuclear processes in stars which enable them to radiate energy at a very high rate for a very long time;

3 appreciate how astronomers have built up a plausible theory of the birth, life and death of stars;

4 describe the stages in the life-history of a star which are represented by main sequence stars, red giants and white dwarfs;

5 demonstrate awareness of other astronomical bodies which theory predicts may be produced when stars die and of the observational evidence for their existence.

The Hertzsprung–Russell (H–R) diagram *(figure 3.4)* incorporates information about the absolute magnitudes, temperatures, sizes and masses of stars. It is essentially a very useful summary of these features of the stars as they now are (or, more correctly, as they were at the time when the radiation now reaching Earth was originally emitted).

However, since stars are radiating energy at a colossal rate, it follows that they cannot continue to do this indefinitely. Stars, like things on Earth, must change with time. Astronomers have long suspected that different groups of stars on the H–R diagram – main sequence stars, red giants and white dwarfs – might represent not so much altogether different *types* of star but rather different *stages* in the life-histories of stars. To be able to interpret the H–R diagram in this way, however, astronomers first needed to understand how stars can radiate energy so fast for so long.

The source of stars' radiant energy

During the second half of the nineteenth century and the early years of the twentieth, explaining the source of the Sun's radiant energy was a particu-larly troublesome problem. By any known chemical or physical process, the Sun had enough mass to release energy at more or less its present rate for only a very small fraction of time needed for either geological or biological evolution to have occurred.

Einstein's theory of special relativity, published in 1905, offered a possible solution to this problem. Scientists had previously believed that, in any closed system, nothing that happens can change either the total mass or the total energy of that system. One of the implications of Einstein's theory, however, is that mass can be converted into energy and vice versa, and that it is the mass-plus-energy of any system which remains constant. Einstein's theory also indicated that mass and energy were related by the formula

$$E = \Delta m c^2$$

where E is energy (J), Δm is change in mass (kg), and c is the velocity of light (m s^{-1}).

Because light travels very quickly (3×10^8 m s^{-1}), a very small loss in mass results in the release of a very large amount of energy. The loss of a small percentage of the Sun's mass, therefore, has allowed it to radiate energy at its present rate for the billions of years scientists have estimated were needed for geological and biological evolution.

SAQ 4.1

How much energy would be released by a loss in mass of 1 g?

SAQ 4.2

The Sun's mass is approximately 2×10^{30} kg. It radiates energy at a rate of 4×10^{26} J s^{-1}. Scientists estimate that the Sun can continue to radiate energy at its present rate until a further 0.035% of its mass has been lost. Calculate how long this will take.

Stimulated by this idea of the inter-convertibility of mass and energy, and by many discoveries about the structure of atoms, physicists gradually developed theories concerning how, at the very high temperatures found in the core of the Sun and other stars, small atomic nuclei might join together – or *fuse* – to produce larger atomic nuclei. They were eventually able to calculate the following details of such **thermonuclear fusion reactions**:

■ which particular atomic nuclei would fuse;
■ the atomic nuclei which would result from these fusions;
■ the minimum temperature at which each fusion reaction would occur;
■ the loss of mass involved and thus the amount of energy released.

For example, the reaction believed to occur in the Sun's core, at a temperature of about 15 million kelvin, is the fusion of hydrogen nuclei (symbol: H^+) to form helium nuclei (symbol: He^{2+}). The net result of this nuclear reaction is:

$$4H^+ \rightarrow He^{2+} + 2 \text{ neutrinos} + 2 \text{ positrons}$$

Positrons are the anti-matter equivalent of electrons so that when a positron encounters an electron they annihilate each other. This very quickly happens to the positrons from the above fusion reaction, the loss of mass from each annihilation resulting in the emission of a photon of gamma radiation. Overall, during this fusion reaction, approximately 0.7% of the initial mass is converted to energy. Because the fusion of hydrogen nuclei releases energy, it is often referred to as **hydrogen burning**. It is important to remember, however, that the nuclear reaction involved is totally different from what is normally meant by burning, i.e. the chemical reaction of combustion.

A very high temperature is needed for this thermonuclear fusion reaction because atomic nuclei are positively charged and must have enough kinetic energy to overcome the increasingly large force of repulsion between them as they are brought closer and closer together. Once the nuclei are sufficiently close, however, a short-range force of attraction known as the **strong force** is able to hold them together. It is, of course, highly unlikely that four hydrogen nuclei will all meet with sufficient energy in the same place and at the same time to fuse and

form a helium nucleus. The reaction actually occurs in several stages *(box 4A)*.

Once physicists had worked out the details of hydrogen burning, and of various other thermo-

Box 4A Hydrogen burning: the thermonuclear reaction in main sequence stars

The main process by which hydrogen nuclei fuse to produce helium nuclei is rather more complicated than the overall equation for the reaction suggests.

First two protons fuse to form a deuterium nucleus *(figure 4.1a)*:

$$^1H^+ + {}^1H^+ \rightarrow {}^2D^+ + \nu + e^+$$

[Note. $^2D^+$ means that a deuterium nucleus has 2 nucleons, i.e. protons+neutrons, and 1 unit of positive electrical charge.]

Then a further proton fuses to produce a helium-3 nucleus *(figure 4.1b)*:

$$^1H^+ + {}^2D^+ \rightarrow {}^3He^{2+}$$

Finally, two helium-3 nuclei fuse producing a helium-4 nucleus and releasing two protons *(figure 4.1c)*:

$$^3He^{2+} + {}^3He^{2+} \rightarrow {}^4He^{2+} + 2{}^1H^+$$

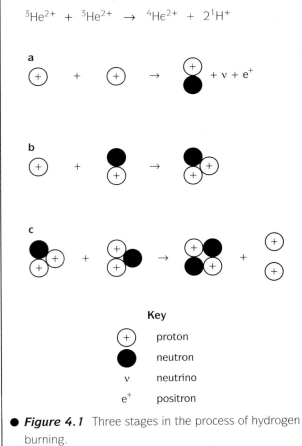

Key

(+)	proton
●	neutron
ν	neutrino
e^+	positron

● *Figure 4.1* Three stages in the process of hydrogen burning.

nuclear fusion reactions occurring at even higher temperatures, astronomers were then able, for the first time, to produce a satisfactory account of the life-histories of stars. Though there is much detail we still do not understand, and though we may need to revise our views in the light of future discoveries, most astronomers believe the account of the life-history of stars which is outlined below to be substantially along the right lines.

The birth and life of a star

What people sometimes think of as empty space in fact contains gas, and it is from this gas that astronomers believe stars are born. The gas is mainly hydrogen, with some helium and smaller amounts of other substances also present. In most regions of space the gas is very thinly dispersed; on average there is just one atom per several hundred cubic metres of space. In some regions of space, however, the gas is rather denser than elsewhere. In such **interstellar gas clouds**, atoms of hydrogen (usually joined in pairs to form molecules) and atoms of helium may be close enough and cool enough – i.e. moving slowly enough – to be drawn together by their

Mass (Sun = 1)	Time on main sequence ($\times 10^6$ years)
0.5	200 000
1	10 000
3	15
25	3

● **Table 4.1** Lifetimes of main sequence stars

gravitational attraction for each other. If, within such a gas cloud, an area develops in which the atoms are rather closer together than in surrounding regions, they will more strongly attract each other. This will result in the density of the gas cloud increasing further so that atoms will not only attract each other even more strongly but will also attract atoms from an increasingly large surrounding region. A positive feedback loop of this kind may eventually produce a **proto-star**, i.e. a local concentration of atoms which is large enough to create a star.

As the atoms in the proto-star are drawn closer together, a reduction in their gravitational potential energy is balanced by an increase in the kinetic energy of their random, disordered movement. In other words, the temperature rises. When the temperature reaches about 3000 kelvin, the nuclei of the hydrogen and helium atoms can no longer hold on to their orbiting electrons, and when the temperature reaches several million kelvin hydrogen burning begins. Once this thermonuclear fusion reaction has ignited, enormous amounts of energy are released and eventually a state of equilibrium is reached in which:

■ the energy radiated by the star exactly balances the energy released by thermonuclear fusion, so that the star maintains a steady temperature;
■ the thermal and radiation pressure acting outwards from the core exactly balances the gravitational pressure tending to collapse the star's mass inwards, so the star maintains a constant size.

The main sequence stars on a Hertzsprung–Russell diagram are in this steady state. Whereas it takes only a relatively short time for stars to form – between ten thousand and a million years, depending on their size – they stay as stable, main sequence stars for much longer. The greater the mass of a star, however, the faster its rate of hydrogen burning and the *shorter* its life as a main sequence star *(table 4.1)*.

It is not possible to see stars being born in interstellar gas clouds because of the dust particles – containing elements other than hydrogen and helium – which are also present. Infrared telescopes, however, penetrate this dust and have provided some direct observational evidence to support the above theory. Once a star is formed, the intense radiation it emits forces away any remaining gases from its immediate surroundings, making the star visible, and also causes a large region of the surrounding gas cloud to glow. The Orion nebula is believed to be the glowing gas cloud surrounding a 'nursery' of young stars *(figure 4.2)*.

SAQ 4.3

What pattern does *table 4.1* suggest about the relationship between the mass of a main sequence star and its rate of hydrogen burning? How could this pattern be explained?

● **Figure 4.2** The Orion nebula: a star nursery. Radiation from the stars which have formed causes the remainder of the gas cloud from which they were created to glow.

SAQ 4.4

If a collapsing mass of gas is less than 0.05 of the Sun's mass, a main sequence star will not be produced. Explain why. What would you expect to be produced?

SAQ 4.5

Where, on an H–R diagram, would you expect a star to be during the period when it is developing into a stable, main sequence star?

Despite the fact that a small loss in mass results in the release of an immense amount of energy, all of the hydrogen in the core of a star will eventually be used up so that it can no longer maintain its stable equilibrium and remain a main sequence star. Hydrogen burning may continue in a shell surrounding the core, but the core itself will contract. As with the initial contraction which formed the star, the reduction in gravitational potential energy is balanced by an increase in kinetic energy, i.e. the temperature of the

core rises. This increases the rate of energy output from the core which then causes the star to expand considerably. As the star expands, its outer layers cool and a type of star known as a red giant is eventually produced *(figure 4.3)*.

SAQ 4.6

On an H–R diagram, variable stars, including Cepheid variables, form a diagonal line from mid-way along the main sequence to the region of the red giants. What does this suggest about variable stars?

As the core of a red giant continues to contract, its temperature eventually rises high enough (around 100 million kelvin) to ignite another thermo-nuclear reaction known as **helium burning**. Helium burning is a multi-stage process.

■ First, two helium nuclei fuse to produce a beryllium nucleus:

$$2He \rightarrow Be$$

■ Next, another helium nucleus is added to produce a carbon nucleus, a photon of gamma (γ) radiation also being emitted:

$$Be + He \rightarrow C + \gamma$$

■ Finally, the carbon nucleus may fuse with a further helium nucleus, to produce an oxygen

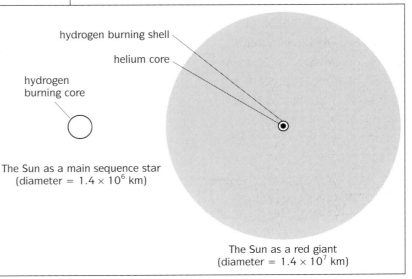

hydrogen burning shell

helium core

hydrogen burning core

The Sun as a main sequence star
(diameter = 1.4×10^6 km)

The Sun as a red giant
(diameter = 1.4×10^7 km)

● **Figure 4.3** The Sun as a red giant.
When the Sun eventually becomes a red giant, its atmosphere will expand to engulf Mercury, Venus and ultimately the Earth itself.

nucleus, again with the emission of gamma radiation:

$$C + He \rightarrow O + \gamma$$

[Note. In the above equations, the nucleon numbers and electrical charges of the atomic nuclei have been omitted.]

Core helium burning can maintain a red giant in a stable state for 10% to 20% of the time it spent as a main sequence star. As with core hydrogen burning, however, all the core helium will eventually be consumed; the equilibrium will then no longer be maintained and the core of the star will collapse once more. What then happens depends on how high the temperature rises as a result of this collapse and this, in turn, depends on the mass of the star. If a star's mass is below a certain critical level, its death is a relatively peaceful affair; if, however, its mass is above the critical level its death is violent and spectacular.

The death of a star

For red giants whose mass is less than about three times the mass of the Sun, the temperature reached in the core after the completion of helium burning will not be high enough to ignite any further thermonuclear reactions. The star will, however, become unstable and shed the outer layers of gas which make up approximately half its mass. This gas may be ionised by the intense radiation from the core. The resulting glow is known as a **planetary nebula** *(figure 4.4)*.

The core of the star continues to collapse into a smaller and smaller space, and become correspondingly more dense, until the electrons – which are responsible for most of the volume of matter as we know it on Earth – are packed closely enough together to generate an effect known as Fermi pressure. This pressure then prevents any further collapse. The eventual result is a very hot star which is very small, typically about 1% of the diameter of the Sun, and which has a very high density, typically 1 tonne cm^{-3}, i.e. several tonnes per teaspoonful. Such stars are the white dwarfs on the Hertzsprung–Russell diagram. White dwarfs are not very bright stars and are difficult to see, even using large telescopes *(figure 4.5)*. They gradually cool, becoming progressively dimmer as they do so.

There is, however, an upper limit to the size of a white dwarf. In 1930, Subramanyan Chandrasekhar calculated that if a white dwarf has a mass greater than 1.4 times the mass of the Sun – a mass now

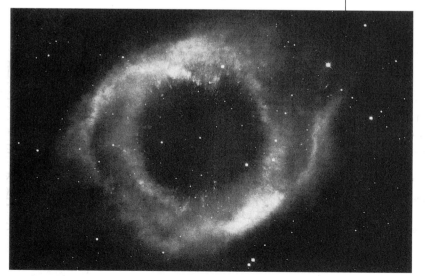

● *Figure 4.4* Helix: a planetary nebula.
The star which produced this nebula can be seen at the exact centre.
[Note. The name 'planetary nebulae' is rather misleading since they have no connection whatsoever with planets. They were thought to resemble planets when first seen through a telescope and the name has stuck.]

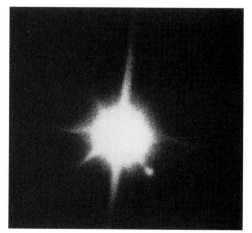

● *Figure 4.5* Sirius and its white dwarf companion.
'Wobbles' in the position of Sirius – the star which looks brighter than any other from Earth – led to the discovery of its binary partner, a white dwarf (at a 5 o'clock position with respect to Sirius in the photograph).

known as the **Chandrasekhar limit** – even the Fermi pressure of electrons will not be able to support the immense gravitational pressure exerted on the core. The electrons will combine with protons in the nuclei of atoms – producing neutrons – and the collapse will then continue until these neutrons are themselves tightly packed. This final collapse will be very rapid – taking less than a second – and will be accompanied by an extremely rapid rise in temperature.

A red giant which is massive enough to collapse beyond the stage of a white dwarf does not do so immediately after the completion of its helium burning. One or more of a series of further thermonuclear reactions first occur, each of which produces an equilibrium and prevents further collapse until its fuel is exhausted *(box 4B)*. Each successive reaction is ignited, however, only if gravitational collapse of the core on completion of the previous thermonuclear reaction produces a sufficiently large increase in temperature.

When the fuel for a red giant's final thermonuclear reaction is exhausted, its collapsing core exceeds the Chandrasekhar limit. The collapse will, therefore, continue until the neutrons of which the core is now exclusively made are themselves compressed as tightly as they will go. The combined effect of the shock wave which is produced when the very rapid final collapse is suddenly brought to a halt and the intense radiation pressure from the immensely hot core then causes the star to explode. The result is known as a **supernova** and may, for a few days, emit as much radiation as a complete galaxy of stable stars before becoming a rather less prominent nebula *(figure 4.6)*.

In the extreme temperatures and pressures which prevail during a supernova explosion, further thermonuclear fusion reactions occur which absorb rather than release energy. This is how the elements with atomic nuclei reactions more massive than iron are created. Nuclei of these elements continue to exist in the debris of the explosion which rapidly cools as it is dispersed into the hydrogen and helium gas in the surrounding region. In the course of time, local density fluctuations and gravitational attraction may then cause these clouds of gas and dust to collapse and so give birth to a new generation of stars.

Box 4B Further thermonuclear reactions in red giants

If the mass of a red giant is great enough, one or more of the following sequence of thermonuclear reactions may occur after helium burning is complete:

- if, after helium burning ceases, the temperature reaches 600 million kelvin, **carbon burning** occurs, producing neon and magnesium nuclei;
- if, after carbon burning ceases, the temperature reaches 1 billion kelvin, **neon burning** occurs, producing oxygen and magnesium nuclei;
- if, after neon burning ceases, the temperature reaches 1.5 billion kelvin, **oxygen burning** occurs, producing a variety of nuclei, including silicon;
- if, after oxygen burning ceases, the temperature approaches 3 billion kelvin, **silicon burning** begins. This involves many nuclear reactions, the final product of which is very stable iron nuclei.

Further nuclear fusion would not result in the release of energy and so does not occur.

Each of the reactions in the series occurs more rapidly than the last, from a few hundred years for carbon burning to around a day for silicon burning.

SAQ 4.7

Explain the most common elements in the Sun *(table 3.2)*.

● *Figure 4.6* The Crab nebula: a supernova first seen in 1054.

Stars, then, change with time. They are born, live out their lives and die, in some cases producing the raw materials from which other stars are born. But if stars have a life-history, what of the Universe as a whole? Has it always been the way it now is or does it, too, have a life-history? If so, how and when did it start and how is it likely to end? These fundamental cosmological questions are examined in chapter 5. First, however, various other types of star, all of which were discovered during the second half of the twentieth century, will briefly be considered.

SAQ 4.8

We know, from spectroscopic analysis, that the Sun contains the nuclei of many elements heavier than iron. What does this indicate about the origin of the Sun?

SAQ 4.9

There are far more main sequence stars than there are red giants or white dwarfs. Why is this?

Neutron stars and black holes

Detailed calculations using computer models suggest that, under certain conditions, part of a star's core might remain intact after a supernova explosion and so form a **neutron star**. Such a star would have a density more than a hundred million times greater than a white dwarf, which itself has a density almost a million times greater than the Earth. A neutron star with the same mass as the Sun would have a diameter of only about 30 kilometres and a teaspoonful of material from it would have a mass of several hundred million tonnes.

Though the *theoretical* existence of neutron stars was clearly suggested by calculations, most astronomers did not, until 1967, believe that they *actually* existed. Some unexpected observations made by the young Cambridge astronomer Jocelyn Bell and her supervisor Antony Hewish were to change all that. Having helped him to set up 2048 dipole antennae covering an area the size of three football pitches (*figure 4.7*), they were using them to survey galaxies which emitted radio waves, i.e. low frequency electromagnetic radiation. The

signals received by the array of antennae were automatically plotted, and one day, when examining the chart, she noticed an unusual looking signal.

On checking back, she found that the signal had occurred several times before. Hewish and Bell then set up special recordings and found that the signal was a series of beeps with a period of 1.337 301 1 seconds, regular to an accuracy of better than a millionth of a second. Careful checks showed that the pulses were not being produced on Earth, for example by electronic equipment. Other pulsating radio sources were also discovered in different areas of the sky, including one in the Crab nebula – a supernova remnant – with a period of one-thirtieth of a second. These pulsating sources of radio-wave radiation were given the name **pulsars**.

● *Figure 4.7* Jocelyn Bell (now Professor Jocelyn Bell-Burnell) and the dipole array.
Note the 'low-tech' nature of the dipole array which led to the discovery of pulsars.

Assuming that the frequency of the pulses corresponds to the frequency at which a pulsar vibrates or rotates, pulsars must be very small bodies. The intensity of the radio signals from pulsars which reach Earth, hundreds of light-years away, suggests that they are also very massive and very dense. The most plausible explanation of pulsars is that they are neutron stars *(box 4C)*.

Box 4C Are pulsars neutron stars?

The Sun rotates approximately once per month. If it collapsed to the size of a neutron star, its angular momentum would remain the same. The huge reduction in diameter would, therefore, greatly increase its rate of rotation. It would, in fact, rotate about once per second, i.e. at approximately the same frequency as the radio pulses from a pulsar.

The Sun, like other stars, has a magnetic field. If the Sun collapsed to the size of a neutron star, its magnetic field would be a billion times stronger. If, as on Earth, the magnetic axis of a neutron star is at an angle to the axis of rotation, the powerful electrical field created would accelerate charged particles along the magnetic axis. This would cause a narrow beam of radiation to be emitted from around each magnetic pole of the neutron star. As the neutron star rotated on its axis these beams of radiation would sweep out a path through space. If the Earth happens to lie on this path, we will receive a short burst of radiation with each rotation of the neutron star.

X-ray detectors on satellites have discovered **X-ray pulsars**. These pulsars regularly switch off for periods of a few hours. This suggests a neutron star which is part of a binary system and is periodically eclipsed by its partner.

X-rays would be produced as gases captured from its main sequence companion collided violently with the neutron star.

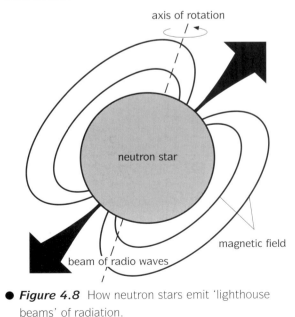

● *Figure 4.8* How neutron stars emit 'lighthouse beams' of radiation.

SAQ 4.10 _____
Explain why it is likely that only a small proportion of pulsars can be detected from Earth.

The theories developed by astrophysicists, about what can happen as burnt-out stars collapse, predict the possibility of a further stage of development beyond a neutron star. If the mass of a neutron star is greater than about three solar masses, neutrons would no longer be able to withstand the immense gravitational pressure and the core of the star would shrink to an infinitesimally small point with an infinitely high density. For a radius of a few kilometres around such a point, the gravitational field would be so strong that not even light and other forms of electromagnetic radiation could escape. We would have what is known as a **black hole**.

As with neutron stars, most astronomers once thought that black holes, though theoretically possible, did not actually exist and left speculation about them to writers of science fiction. Though we cannot, by definition, ever see a black hole, we should, if they exist, be able to detect their effects. There are, in fact, a number of observations which suggest that black holes do exist. First, mass calculations for some binary stars suggest that the 'invisible partner' is too massive to be either a white dwarf or a neutron star and might, therefore, be a black hole. Secondly, many very bright sources of radiation in the radio-wave region of the electromagnetic spectrum have been observed by radio astronomers. The intense radiation emitted by these quasi-stellar radio sources, or **quasars** *(box 4D)*, may be produced as matter is accelerated in the very powerful gravitational field surrounding a black hole. Thirdly, the intense radio-frequency emission from the centre of our own galaxy could be caused by gases rapidly orbiting a very massive yet relatively small body such as a black hole. Fourthly, powerful X-ray sources, for example Cygnus X-1, may be produced by binary systems in which one member is a main sequence star and the other a black hole. As gases from the main sequence star spiral in towards the black hole they would reach a sufficiently high velocity for X-rays to be emitted.

The pulsar in the Crab nebula also pulses in the visible region of the electromagnetic spectrum. The 30 Hz flashes are, however, too rapid to be detected by the human eye. Suggest how they might be detected.

Box 4D Quasars

Before the development of radio astronomy during the 1940s, everything astronomers knew about the Universe was based on visual observations.

One of the first very strong radio-wave sources to be discovered, known as Cygnus A, was estimated (by the red-shift method described in chapter 5) to be a billion light-years distant. This meant the radio-brightness of Cygnus A was 10 million times greater than that of an average galaxy. Many more of these radio-wave sources have been discovered, with massive red-shifts implying distances of up to 18 billion light-years and with optical brightnesses up to 100 times greater than the brightest galaxies. It was because these extraordinary sources were quite unlike any other stars astronomers had ever seen that they were called *quasi*-stellar radio sources, or **quasars**.

Astronomers later discovered that many quasars fluctuated in brightness with periods varying from a few months to a few days. Since an object cannot vary in brightness in a shorter time than it takes for light to travel across it, a quasar might be only a few light-days in diameter and yet be many times brighter than a galaxy. If quasars really are as distant as their red-shifts imply, their huge power output in relation to their small size cannot easily be explained except in terms of the radiation emitted by matter as it rapidly orbits and/or is sucked into a black hole.

SUMMARY

■ Stars can emit intense radiation for very long periods of time because of the thermonuclear fusion reactions which occur in their cores. In these reactions:
  ● small atomic nuclei join to produce larger atomic nuclei;
  ● there is a fractional loss in mass which results in the release of a large amount of energy, according to the relationship $E = \Delta m c^2$.

■ Main sequence stars are born as the gases (mainly hydrogen and helium) and dust in interstellar clouds are drawn together by gravitational forces. Loss in gravitational potential energy causes an increase in the kinetic energy of atomic nuclei, i.e. a rise in temperature.

■ During its life on the main sequence, a star is in equilibrium:
  ● energy released by hydrogen burning in the core balances energy emitted as radiation, so a steady temperature is maintained;
  ● gravitational pressure tending to collapse the core is balanced by thermal and radiation pressure tending to expand it, so a constant size is maintained.

■ Once the hydrogen in a star's core is all converted to helium, it begins to collapse again under gravitational pressure.

■ The subsequent life-history of a star depends on its mass *(figure 4.11)*.

■ Evidence for the existence of immensely dense neutron stars, and of even denser black holes from which not even electromagnetic radiation can escape, includes:
  ● pulsars, whose rapidly pulsing radio waves could be produced by rapidly rotating neutron stars;
  ● quasars, whose immensely bright radiation from a very small source could be explained if they were powered by the gravitational field of a black hole;
  ● powerful X-ray sources which could be produced in a binary system as gases from a main sequence star spiral into its black hole partner.

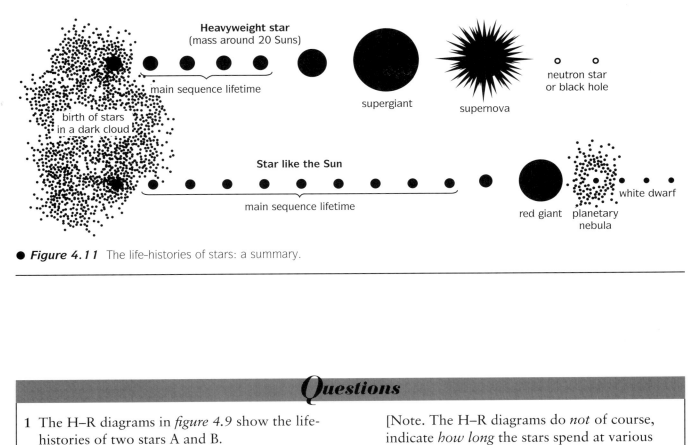

● *Figure 4.11* The life-histories of stars: a summary.

Questions

1 The H–R diagrams in *figure 4.9* show the life-histories of two stars A and B.

Describe the life-histories of the two stars and suggest an explanation of the differences between them.

[Note. The H–R diagrams do *not* of course, indicate *how long* the stars spend at various stages of their life-history.]

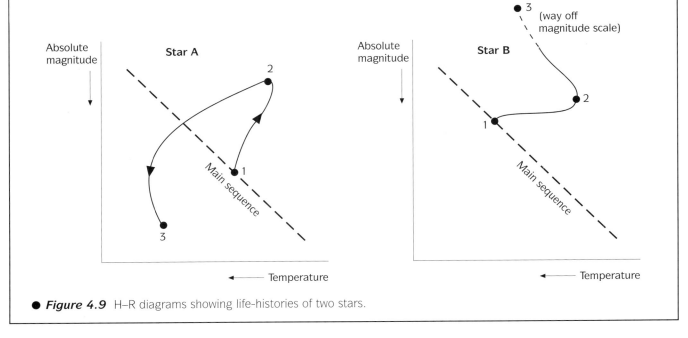

● *Figure 4.9* H–R diagrams showing life-histories of two stars.

Questions

2 a Stars tend to occur in clusters, all the stars in the same cluster being approximately the same age. The H–R diagram for the stars in a cluster often gives an indication of its age *(figure 4.10)*. Put the clusters X, Y and Z in order of age, from the youngest to the oldest. Give reasons for your answer.

b The spectral lines in the stars form young clusters shows that they are metal-rich. these stars are known as Population I stars. Stars from older clusters have spectra with only very weak absorption lines for metal elements. These Population II stars are metal-poor.

Suggest an explanation for these differences.

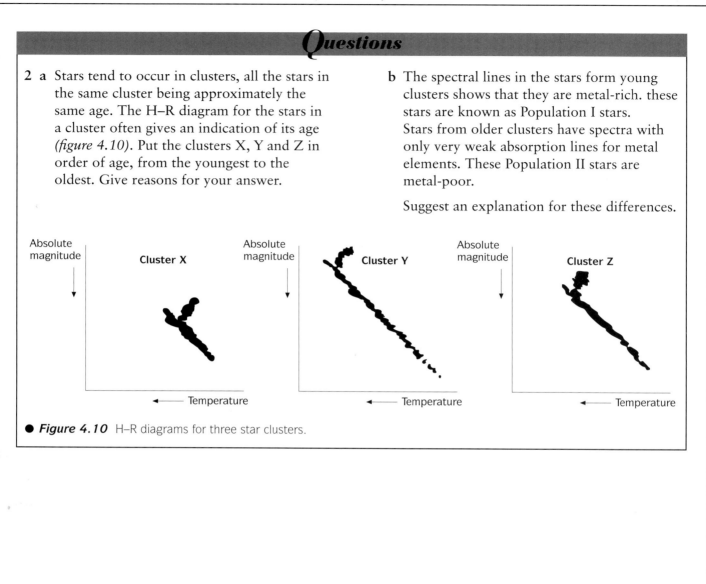

● *Figure 4.10* H–R diagrams for three star clusters.

Chapter five

The origin and future of the Universe

By the end of this chapter you should be able to:

1 explain why older cosmological theories involving an unchanging Universe have been superseded by the standard – hot big bang – model;

2 understand how the age of the Universe can be estimated;

3 describe the key stages in the development of the Universe from the start of the big bang to the present day;

4 describe the range of possibilities for the future of the Universe and explain the factors that determine which will actually occur.

By the mid-1920s, Hubble's distance measurements had confirmed a model of the Universe in which stars were grouped into galaxies, and local clusters of galaxies themselves were distributed uniformly in space. Though galaxies more than 500 million light-years away were too faint to be seen, there was no reason to believe that the Universe did not continue in the same way beyond that distance. In other words, astronomers had established a cosmological model which was fully compatible with Newton's view of a static, uniform and infinite Universe existing in the framework of absolute space. Within the next few years, however, this model was shown to be seriously flawed.

Olbers' paradox

One serious problem with Newton's cosmological model had been pointed out as early as 1826 by Heinrich Olbers. Olbers showed that in an infinite, uniform Universe the sky at night would be exceedingly bright (box 5A), whereas we know perfectly well that this is not so. This contradiction – that the Universe must be infinite otherwise it would collapse under its own gravitational forces, yet cannot be infinite otherwise the sky would be bright at night – is now known as **Olbers' paradox**.

SAQ 5.1

Explain, as fully as you can, why a static Universe must also be infinite.

Box 5A Olbers' paradox

In its simplest form, the argument that the night sky in an infinite Universe would be bright is based on the idea that along any particular line of sight there would eventually be a star. Since most of these stars would be extremely dim, however, this argument is not very convincing. The following argument is very much better.

Imagine a thin shell in space at a radius r from Earth. Radiation from the stars in this shell will reach the Earth with a small, but definite, intensity. Imagine also a second shell, the same thickness as the first but at twice the distance, i.e. with a radius of $2r$.

In a uniform Universe, the stars in the larger shell will, on average, be the same distance apart and will radiate energy at the same rate as the stars in the smaller shell. However, because of its greater distance:

● the average intensity of radiation reaching Earth from each star in the larger shell will be only one-quarter of that from the smaller shell (inverse square law);

● the volume of the larger shell will be four times greater than the smaller shell, so it will contain four times as many stars.

Overall, therefore, the intensity of radiation reaching Earth from each shell will be exactly the same.

A similar argument applies to any thin shell, whatever its distance from Earth. In an infinite Universe, there is an infinite number of such shells of stars. However small the intensity of radiation received from each shell, therefore, the total intensity of radiation received will be infinitely large.

Even when allowance is made for nearby stars intercepting some of the radiation from more distant stars, the radiation level on Earth ought nevertheless to be about as high as it is on the surface of an average star, e.g. the Sun.

If an argument begins with certain assumptions and, by correct reasoning, arrives at a conclusion which is false, there must be something wrong with the assumptions. In order to arrive at the conclusion that the sky could not be dark at night, Olbers, like Newton, not only assumed that the Universe is infinite and uniform but also made two further assumptions:

■ first, that space extends indefinitely in all directions, as a sort of invisible three-dimensional grid, quite independently of any matter – stars, gas clouds, galaxies etc. – which might happen to be present;
■ secondly, that the Universe is static.

Astronomers now believe both of these assumptions to be incorrect. The reasons for the rejection of the idea of absolute space are considered in chapter 6. Olbers' paradox itself, however, was resolved by Hubble's discovery, in 1929, that the Universe is not static but expanding.

Hubble's law

Hubble made this discovery from his detailed measurements of the spectra produced by the light from other galaxies. Vesto Slipher had previously discovered that the dark lines in these spectra, although clearly identifiable as indicating particular elements, were slightly out of position, usually shifted towards the red end of the spectrum (*figure 5.1*). Slipher explained these **red-shifts** in terms of the **Doppler effect** *(box 5B)*: the increase in the wavelength of the spectral lines meant that our own galaxy and other galaxies were moving away from each other.

Furthermore, the bigger a galaxy's red-shift, the greater its **speed of recession**, i.e. the faster a galaxy and the Earth are moving apart. In fact, for speeds of recession which are small compared to the speed of light, the fractional change in the wavelength ($\Delta\lambda/\lambda$) is equal to the speed of galaxy (v) expressed as a fraction of the speed of light (c):

$$\Delta\lambda/\lambda = v/c$$

An example

Galaxy A on *figure 5.1* has its dark H and K calcium lines red-shifted by 0.4%. This indicates that it is moving away from Earth at 0.4% of the speed of light.

Since

$$\frac{v}{c} = \frac{0.4}{100}$$

then

$$v = \frac{0.4}{100} c$$

$$= \frac{0.4}{100} \times 3 \times 10^8 \,\mathrm{m\,s^{-1}}$$

$$= 1.2 \times 10^6 \,\mathrm{m\,s^{-1}}$$

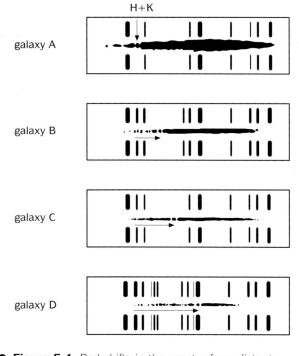

● *Figure 5.1* Red-shifts in the spectra from distant galaxies.
The horizontal arrows show the red-shifts of the calcium H and K lines in the spectra for galaxies B, C and D. On the scale the spectra are shown on this page, the red-shift for galaxy A is 0.6 mm, which represents a fractional change in wavelength ($\Delta\lambda/\lambda$) of 0.004.

SAQ 5.2

How fast are the other galaxies shown on *figure 5.1* moving away from Earth?

Box 5B The Doppler effect

The change in wavelength due to relative motion between a source and an observer was first explained by Christian Doppler, in 1841.

Consider a source emitting light with a wavelength of λ metres and travelling at c metres per second.

The time taken for one complete wave to be emitted is then λ/c seconds *(figure 5.2a)*.

If the source is moving with a speed of v metres per second, it will have moved away from the observer by a distance of $v \times \lambda/c$ metres during the time it takes for one complete wave to be emitted *(figure 5.2b)*.

This means that the wavelength of the light as seen by the observer will have been increased by this amount *(figure 5.2c)*.

The change in wavelength $\Delta\lambda$ is given by

$$\Delta\lambda = v \times \lambda/c$$

and the fractional change in wavelength by

$$\Delta\lambda/\lambda = v/c$$

The same relationship applies if the source and observer are moving towards each other, except that in this case the wavelength of the light is reduced.

[Note. The above argument is an approximation which is strictly valid only as the value of v/c tends to zero.]

a Source emits 1 complete wave in $\frac{\lambda}{c}$ seconds.

b As it does so, the source moves back by $v \times \frac{\lambda}{c}$ metres.

c So the wavelength is stretched by $v \times \frac{\lambda}{c}$.

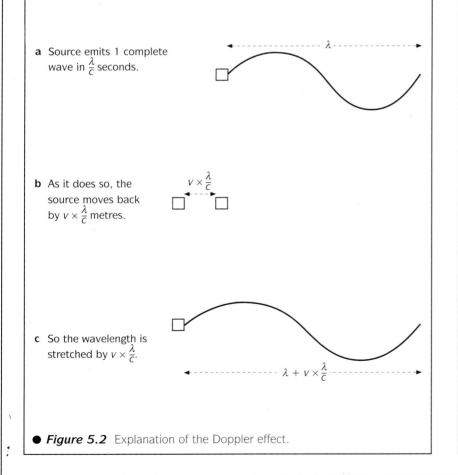

● **Figure 5.2** Explanation of the Doppler effect.

SAQ 5.3

The first astronomer to measure a speed using the Doppler effect was Sir William Huggins in 1868. He found that the dark lines in the spectrum of the star Sirius were red-shifted by 1/10 000 of their normal wavelengths. What does this tell us about Sirius?

SAQ 5.4

In 1912, Slipher showed that light from the nearby Andromeda galaxy is slightly *blue*-shifted. What does this indicate? Suggest why the movement of Andromeda relative to Earth should be different from the movement of most other galaxies.

By measuring the distances and red-shifts of a large number of galaxies, Hubble discovered a pattern in the recessional speeds of galaxies: the further away a galaxy is, the faster its speed of recession. More precisely, the recessional speed is directly proportional to its distance from Earth *(figure 5.3)*. This relationship is called **Hubble's law** and implies that the whole Universe is expanding.

The fact that the Universe is expanding offers a solution to Olbers' paradox. Light – like other forms of electromagnetic radiation – is radiated as small 'packets', or **quanta**, of energy called photons. If a galaxy and the Earth are moving apart, the number of photons reaching the Earth each second from that galaxy is reduced. Furthermore, the red-shift associated with recession also means that the energy of each individual photon is smaller.

Since the rate at which galaxies move apart increases with

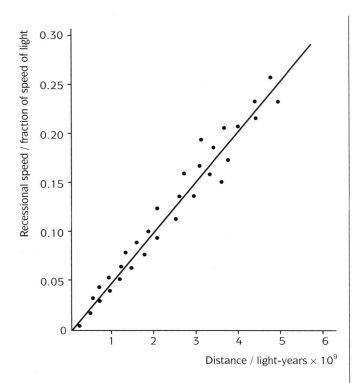

● **Figure 5.3** Hubble's law.
[Note. Hubble was not aware of the existence of two types of Cepheid variable (see *figure 2.5*) so that his distances to galaxies were less than half of the corrected distances shown on the graph.]

distance, each of the above effects also increases with distance. This means that the more distant a region of the Universe is, the smaller the contribution it makes to the total amount of light we receive. The total amount of radiation we receive on Earth, therefore, is quite small. In short, it is dark at night because the Universe is expanding.

At first sight, Hubble's law might seem to reverse the Copernican revolution and put the Earth, once again, at the very centre of the Universe. However, a simple thought-experiment *(box 5C)* shows that Hubble's law would apply to the observations of red-shifts from *anywhere* in the Universe: wherever we were in the Universe, other galaxies would recede at speeds directly proportional to their distance and it would seem to us that we were at the centre of the Universe.

The idea of the 'big bang'

The fact that the Universe is expanding not only resolved Olbers' paradox but also suggested when, and how, the Universe began.

Hubble showed that galaxies are moving apart at a speed which is directly proportional to the distance between them (Hubble's law). If we assume that galaxies have always been moving

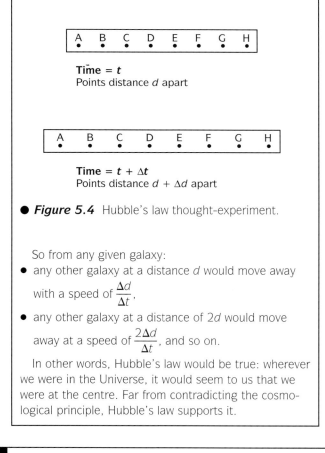

Box 5C Hubble's law and the cosmological principle

Hubble's law – the idea that each part of the Universe is expanding at a rate which is proportional to its distance from Earth – might seem, at first sight, to contradict the cosmological principle, i.e. that everywhere in the Universe is essentially the same. A simple thought-experiment, however, shows that there is, in fact, no contradiction.

If the Universe is expanding uniformly, and in a given period of time Δt any two galaxies initially a distance d apart move a distance Δd further apart, then:
● any two galaxies initially a distance $2d$ apart would move $2\Delta d$ further apart,
● any two galaxies initially a distance $3d$ apart would move $3\Delta d$ further apart, and so on.

Time = t
Points distance d apart

Time = $t + \Delta t$
Points distance $d + \Delta d$ apart

● **Figure 5.4** Hubble's law thought-experiment.

So from any given galaxy:
● any other galaxy at a distance d would move away with a speed of $\dfrac{\Delta d}{\Delta t}$,
● any other galaxy at a distance of $2d$ would move away at a speed of $\dfrac{2\Delta d}{\Delta t}$, and so on.

In other words, Hubble's law would be true: wherever we were in the Universe, it would seem to us that we were at the centre. Far from contradicting the cosmological principle, Hubble's law supports it.

apart at the speeds we now observe, there must have been a time, long ago, when all the galaxies in the Universe were in the same place. In other words, the Universe must have begun with an immense explosion or **big bang**. Furthermore, it is possible to calculate, from Hubble's measurements, when this big bang occurred.

For example, using the information from *figure 5.3*, a galaxy 5×10^9 light-years distant is receding at 0.25 the speed of light.

Since

$$\text{time taken} = \frac{\text{distance travelled}}{\text{speed}}$$

and assuming the galaxy's speed has remained unchanged

$$\text{time taken} = \frac{5 \times 10^9}{0.25}$$

$$= 2 \times 10^{10} \text{ years}$$

In other words, the big bang occurred about 20 billion years ago.

This figure is, however, likely to be a little too high because the speeds at which galaxies are moving apart will have decreased since the big bang due to their gravitational attraction for each other. Taking this into account, most astronomers believe the big bang to have occurred between 15 and 18 billion years ago. Because of its importance in calculating the age of the Universe, astronomers wish to have as accurate a value as possible for the gradient of the Hubble law graph. This value is referred to as the **Hubble constant** *(box 5D)*.

SAQ 5.5

The age of the Universe can be calculated from any point on a Hubble graph. Explain why this is.

SAQ 5.6

Summarise the different ways in which an expanding Universe can provide a solution for Olbers' paradox.

SAQ 5.7

Astronomers often quote Hubble's constant in $\text{km s}^{-1} \text{Mpc}^{-1}$ [M = mega, i.e. 10^6]. If its value in these units is 80, estimate the age of the Universe. [Hint. Convert km s^{-1} to a fraction of c, and Mpc to light-years.]

Box 5D The Hubble constant

Hubble's law can be stated in the form:

$$\frac{\text{speed of recession}}{\text{distance}} = H_0$$

where H_0 is a constant known as the Hubble constant.

The value of this constant can be calculated using any part of the graph in *figure 5.3*. For example:

$$H_0 = \frac{0.25}{5 \times 10^9}$$

and since a fraction of the speed of light is being divided by light-years the unit of the Hubble constant in this case is year^{-1}.

The expression used to calculate the Hubble constant is the inverse of that used to estimate the age of the Universe.

In other words:

$$\text{the age of the universe} = \frac{1}{H_0}$$

[Note. The scales on the graph in *figure 5.3* are not Hubble's. They have been corrected in the light of the discovery by Walter Baade, in 1952, that there are two types of Cepheid variable, each with its own relationship between absolute magnitude and period.]

The idea that the Universe began with a big bang long ago was supported by the discovery, in 1965, of **cosmic microwave background radiation**. Arno Penzias and Robert Wilson were studying the radiation from stars in the microwave region of the electromagnetic spectrum. They found that the microwave detector they were testing was picking up a lot of stray, unwanted radiation or 'noise' which would mask the signals they wanted to pick up when they pointed their detector towards particular galaxies. They checked their apparatus for faults and cleaned dirt – including bird droppings! – from the dish which collected the signals but still the noise was there. Then they tried pointing their dish in different directions but this didn't make any difference either. Penzias and Wilson then realised that the noise wasn't just a problem with their apparatus, but that they had discovered something important. If the noise was just the same from all directions then it must be coming from outside the Earth's atmosphere. By making careful measurements of the noise, they also discovered that the radiation was also the same strength – to within 0.01% (one part in ten thousand) – not only in all directions, but also at all times of day and night and at all times of the year. The intensity of the microwave radiation was not, therefore, affected either by the Earth's spin or by the movement of the Earth in its orbit around the Sun. The radiation must be coming from outside our own galaxy.

The existence of this microwave background radiation pervading the whole Universe, together with the fact that its energy profile corresponded to a black-body temperature of 2.7 K *(box 5E)*, strongly supported the idea that the Universe began with a big bang. At an early stage of the big bang, the Universe would have been very hot and would, therefore, have been pervaded by high-energy radiation which had correspondingly short wavelengths. Because of the huge expansion of the Universe since that time, this radiation would have been 'stretched' to a much longer wavelength, and correspondingly low energy. In fact, about twenty years earlier, George Gamow had predicted, from the big bang theory, that there should be a microwave background radiation corresponding to a black-body temperature just a few kelvin above absolute zero. A group of cosmologists had begun actively to search for this radiation when they heard of its 'accidental' discovery by Penzias and Wilson.

SAQ 5.8

Calculate the wavelength at which the 2.7 K background radiation of the Universe has its maximum intensity.

SAQ 5.9

Explain why the existence of microwave background radiation supports the cosmological principle.

The idea that the Universe as a whole was very hot at an early stage of its development also solved another problem which had been worrying astronomers, namely the amount of helium in the Universe. Overall, the visible matter in the Universe is approximately 70% hydrogen and 27% helium, with all other elements together making up the rest. During the 15–18 billion years the

Universe has existed, hydrogen burning in stars could have converted no more than 2–3% of the hydrogen in the Universe into helium. According to the hot big bang theory, however, the remaining helium could have been produced at the stage of the big bang when the temperature of the Universe as a whole was within the range at which hydrogen burning occurs.

Box 5E The black-body temperature of microwave background radiation

The microwave background radiation first discovered by Penzias and Wilson had a wavelength of about 7 cm. To be able to calculate its black-body temperature, they needed to find the wavelength for which the radiation has its greatest intensity (λ_{max}). Unfortunately, this turned out to be at a wavelength which is strongly absorbed by the Earth's atmosphere. As *figure 5.5* indicates, however, it was still possible to show that the microwave background radiation corresponds to a black-body temperature of 2.7 K.

The Cosmic Background Explorer Satellite (COBE), launched in 1989, which has measured the energy profile of the background radiation very accurately at millimetre wavelengths, indicates a black-body temperature of 2.735 K. Very small variations ('ripples') in the intensity of the radiation have also been detected. The significance of these ripples is considered below.

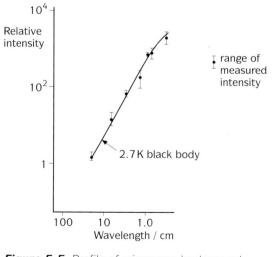

● *Figure 5.5* Profile of microwave background radiation.
Measurements of the relative intensity of the microwave background radiation at wavelengths between 1 cm and 20 cm fit the radiation curve for a black-body temperature of 2.7 K quite closely.

Once the hot big bang theory had become sufficiently well established to be regarded as the **standard model** of the Universe, cosmologists turned their attention to two further matters: first, to working out the details of how the Universe developed from the outset of the big bang into its present form; and secondly, to deciding what the future of the Universe is likely to be.

The Universe from the big bang to the present day

The basic principles of the big bang theory are very simple:

- the Universe was initially exceedingly small and exceedingly hot;
- since the big bang, the Universe has been continually expanding and its temperature continually decreasing.

Cosmologists believe that all the hydrogen and helium from which stars and galaxies eventually developed had been produced by the time the Universe was just a few minutes old and its temperature had fallen to a few million kelvin.

It then took a further million years or so before the temperature fell to 3000 K and the hydrogen and helium nuclei combined with electrons to produce atoms, followed, in the case of hydrogen, by pairs of atoms forming molecules. Once the sea of free electrons was removed from the Universe, photons no longer constantly collided with them so that electromagnetic radiation could travel large distances unimpeded by matter. The Universe became transparent.

From about a million years after the big bang until the present time, the main developments in the Universe have been due to gravitational forces. Whenever the density of hydrogen and helium gases in any particular region of the Universe became slightly greater than in surrounding regions, the effects of gravity further increased this difference in density so that the matter in the Universe became 'lumpy'. Smaller lumps developed in a similar way within larger lumps, and so on. Such clumping on a relatively small scale resulted in the birth of stars as described in chapter 4. Clumping on a bigger scale caused stars to be concentrated into galaxies and the galaxies themselves to form clusters *(figure 5.6)*.

For matter to organise itself in the manner described above, the early Universe could not have been completely uniform. Some slight non-uniformities must have existed and these should still be present as variations in the microwave background radiation. Very small 'ripples' in the background radiation – corresponding to variations in temperature of just 3×10^{-5} of one kelvin – were detected by the Cosmic Background Explorer satellite (COBE) in 1992.

Once they had constructed a plausible account of how the Universe developed from the point when the original hydrogen and helium had been produced, cosmologists increasingly turned their attention to what happened before that point. At first sight, it might seem quite impossible to find out anything about what happened during the first

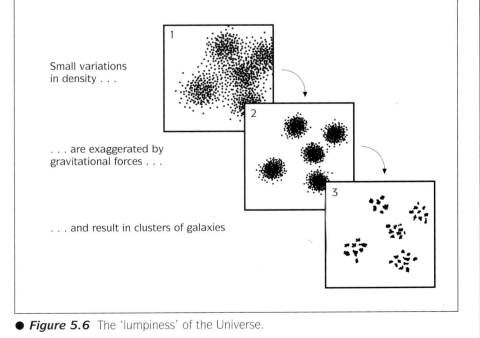

1

Small variations in density . . .

2

. . . are exaggerated by gravitational forces . . .

3

. . . and result in clusters of galaxies

● *Figure 5.6* The 'lumpiness' of the Universe.

few minutes of the Universe. Although we obviously cannot observe what happened during this very early period of the Universe, the discoveries made by *particle physicists* tell us a great deal about what may well have happened.

The first few minutes of the big bang

During the second half of the twentieth century, most of the progress in physicists' understanding of the fundamental particles from which all matter is made, have come from accelerating particles to very high speeds and observing what happens when they collide *(box 5F)*. Since temperature is a measure of the kinetic energy of particles, finding out how particles behave when they collide at very high speeds is, in effect, finding out what happens to them at very high temperatures. Speeds have been reached in particle accelerators which are equivalent to about 10^{15} K, the temperature of the Universe about 10^{-12} of a second after the big bang. Though physicists have no *experimental evidence* for higher temperatures – and hence earlier times – than this, the *theories* they have developed to explain their observations suggest what might happen at even higher temperatures. These things may also have happened at times very close to the start of the big bang.

It is easier to understand what probably happened during the early stages of the big bang by working backwards from what we know about the basic structure of matter at ordinary temperatures and explaining what physicists have discovered happens to this structure as the temperature increases to higher and higher levels. During the big bang, the same sequence of changes would have occurred, but in the opposite direction.

At ordinary temperatures, the basic building blocks of matter are atoms, which are held together in various ways to produce millions of different substances. Each atom itself comprises a nucleus of protons and neutrons together with as many negatively charged orbiting electrons in the immediately surrounding space as there are positively charged protons in the nucleus.

At temperatures greater than about 10^4 K, nuclei can no longer hold on to their orbiting electrons so that matter no longer exists as atoms but as nuclei in a sea of electrons. The core of the Sun and other stars consists of a dense mixture of nuclei and electrons moving around largely independently of each other; this mix is known as **plasma**.

At temperatures greater than about 10^7 K, nuclei themselves are no longer stable and split up into their component protons and neutrons. Matter at this temperature comprises a turbulent sea of protons, neutrons and electrons.

Protons and neutrons are currently believed to be made from fundamental particles called **quarks** and, at temperatures above about 10^{13} K, these quarks can no longer be held together, or **confined**, as protons and neutrons.

As the temperature rises even further, physicists believe that the four types of force which exist in the Universe *(box 5G)* become progressively indistinguishable from each other: at 10^{15} K, the weak and electromagnetic forces merge and, at still higher temperatures, first the strong force and then the gravitational force are no longer identifiable as separate forces. 'Messenger' particles are believed to be responsible for each of these forces and, in 1983, evidence for W and Z bosons – the messenger particles for the weak force – was obtained in a particle accelerator by colliding protons and anti-protons at speeds corresponding to a temperature of 10^{15} K.

At temperatures above 10^{15} K, physicists believe that massless but highly energetic particles, e.g.

Box 5F Particle accelerators

To study the effects of particle collisions at very high speeds – i.e. at very high kinetic energies corresponding to very high temperatures – large and expensive particle accelerators are needed. The electron/positron accelerator at the Centre for European Nuclear Research (CERN) in Geneva, for example, has a circumference of 27 km and cost almost £0.5 billion to build.

Because the mass of particles increases with their speed (see chapter 6), each successive increase in the speed of particles becomes more difficult – and more expensive – to produce.

Box 5G Four types of force

Physicists believe that there are just four different types of force which operate in the Universe. These forces, their major effects and the 'messenger' particles by means of which they are believed to operate are shown in *table 5.1*.

Force	Effect of force	Messenger particle	Mass (proton = 1)
gravity	mainly between large masses and on a large scale	graviton	0
strong	holds protons and neutrons together (both internally and in atomic nuclei)	gluon	0
electro-magnetic	holds electrons in the region around atomic nuclei	photon	0
weak	involved in radioactive decay	W and Z bosons	about 90

● *Table 5.1* The four types of force

photons, are constantly being converted into particles which do possess mass, i.e. into matter, and vice versa. The 'exchange rate' for these energy–mass inter-conversions, like those in nuclear fusion reactions, is given by the relationship

$$E = \Delta m\, c^2$$

As the temperature increases beyond $10^{15}\,\text{K}$, there is a structureless chaos within which increasingly higher energy photons inter-convert with particles of increasingly greater mass.

Cosmologists have combined the physicists' account of what happens to matter as the temperature rises with their own estimates of when the Universe is likely to have been at each of the critical temperatures to construct the history of the Universe, summarised in *table 5.2*.

SAQ 5.10

Suggest an appropriate time to take as the end of the big bang. Give reasons for your answer.

SAQ 5.11

How far back to the beginning of the big bang is there any experimental evidence to support the cosmologists' story of the Universe?

Before leaving the story of the early stages of the big bang one further problem needs to be considered, namely why there is any matter in the Universe at all. This problem arises because physicists have plenty of evidence which indicates that whenever a photon produces a particular particle of matter, i.e. a particle which has mass, the corresponding **anti-particle** is also produced. Should the particle and anti-particle then meet, they annihilate each other, their mass being converted back into a photon of energy:

photon ↔ particle + anti-particle

Below a certain temperature, however, photons will no longer produce particle/anti-particle pairs though such pairs are still annihilated when they meet. All conversions are now in the direction mass → energy:

particle + anti-particle → photon

When the Universe reached this critical temperature, therefore, most of the matter and anti-matter would be annihilated. A massive annihilation of this kind would explain why there are of the order of a billion photons in the Universe for each proton. Since particles and their anti-particles were originally created in equal numbers, however, there remains the problem of why matter was not completely annihilated.

One of the grand unified theories (GUTs), developed by physicists to unify the different types of force, suggests that an asymmetry in the decay of massive X-particles and their anti-particles at a very early, very hot, stage of the Universe might have resulted in an extremely small excess of

Time from big bang (seconds)	Temperature (K)	Key features
0	infinite	A singularity – infinitesimally small, infinitely dense
		All forces unified | Gravitational force freezes out | Strong force freezes out
10^{-12}	10^{15}	Weak and electromagnetic forces freeze out
10^{-6}	10^{14}	Quarks and leptons (e.g. electrons) freeze out
10^{-3}	10^{12}	Quarks confined as e.g. protons and neutrons
10^{2}	10^{7}	Helium nuclei formed by fusion (but too cold for further fusion reactions)
(years) 10^{5}	10^{4} | | | |	Atoms formed as hydrogen nuclei (protons) and helium nuclei combine with electrons Photons travel freely without frequent electron collisions. Universe now transparent
10^{6}	10^{3} | | | | |	Density fluctuations result in clumping of matter at several different scales
1.5–1.8×10^{10}	2.7	Present-day black-body temperature of cosmic background microwave radiation

● **Table 5.2** The history of the Universe. [Note. The relationships between times, temperatures and key features as estimated by different cosmologists differ. The figures given in the table are typical.]

matter over anti-matter *(box 5H)*. This would then explain the small amount of matter remaining in the Universe after the massive annihilation of matter and anti-matter had occurred.

SAQ 5.12

A less energetic photon is needed to create an electron/positron pair than to create a proton/anti-proton pair. Explain why this is so.

SAQ 5.13

Just after the annihilation of matter and anti-matter, the Universe was still dominated by radiation. Now it is dominated by matter. Explain why.

Box 5H Why there is matter in the Universe

Theoretical physicists have suggested the following explanation for the existence of matter in the Universe.

- At a very early stage in the big bang highly energetic photons created massive X-particle/X-anti-particle pairs and vice versa.
- As the temperature fell, the unstable X-particles and X-anti-particles decayed.
- In each case there were two possible decay routes:

  X-particle → quark + quark   or
  $\qquad\qquad$ anti-quark + anti-lepton

  X-anti-particle → anti-quark + anti-quark   or
  $\qquad\qquad$ quark + lepton

  [Note. Electrons belong to the group of particles known as **leptons**.]

- The proportion of X-particles which decayed into quarks was about 1 part in a billion bigger than the proportion of X-anti-particles which decayed into anti-quarks. This meant that there were more quarks than anti-quarks and more leptons than anti-leptons.
- The mutual annihilation of matter and anti-matter, i.e. of lepton/anti-lepton pairs and of quark/anti-quark pairs (or of proton/anti-proton pairs formed from these quarks and anti-quarks), resulted in photons and protons being produced in the ratio of a billion to one.

The future of the Universe

The rate at which galaxies are moving apart must decrease with time due to their gravitational attraction for each other. What eventually happens in the future will, therefore, depend on just how big the gravitational attraction is compared to the rate at which the Universe is expanding. The size of the gravitational attraction is itself determined by the average density of the matter in the Universe.

If the average density of the Universe is below a certain level, known as the **critical density**, then the associated gravitational attraction will be too small ever to stop the Universe from expanding. The Universe would be **open** or **unbounded** *(figure 5.7a)*.

Alternatively, if the average density of the Universe is greater than the critical density, the Universe will eventually stop expanding and begin to contract again. This contraction would accelerate and eventually produce a **big crunch**, the inverse of a big bang. The Universe would be **closed** or **bounded** *(figure 5.7b)*.

A third possibility is that the average density of the Universe is exactly equal to the critical density. Though the expansion of the Universe would, in this case, never stop, it would approach more and more closely to a definite limit. The Universe would be **flat** or **marginally bounded**.

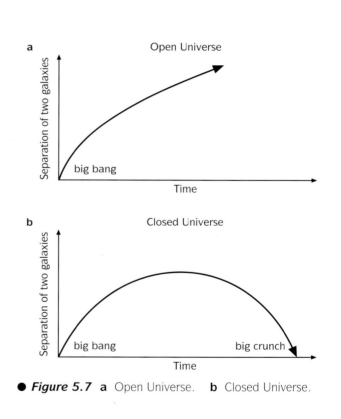

● *Figure 5.7* **a** Open Universe.   **b** Closed Universe.

SAQ 5.14

Make a copy of *figure 5.7b* and extend it to show what might happen after a big crunch.

In order to decide which of these possible futures is likely to occur, cosmologists need to know exactly how the average density of the Universe compares to its critical density. Unfortunately, neither of these figures is very accurately known. The critical density can be calculated from the Hubble constant *(box 5I)*, but there is a considerable margin of error in the measurement of galactic distances and hence of the Hubble constant itself. There is even greater uncertainty concerning the average density of the Universe: not only is it difficult to make an accurate estimate of the visible matter in the Universe, but there is also the question of just how much other matter there is. Some cosmologists believe that such **dark matter** comprises up to 90% of the mass of the Universe. Current estimates suggest that the average density of the Universe and its critical density differ by only a small factor. Though this makes it difficult to decide whether the Universe is open or closed, it also suggests that it might be flat.

In principle, it should be possible to determine whether the Universe is open, flat or closed by measuring the rate at which the Hubble constant varies with distance. The light from very distant galaxies set out earlier in the history of the Universe when the Hubble constant would have

had a higher value. Unfortunately, however, the margin of error involved in measuring the 'constant' (which, strictly speaking, is not a constant at all, but a parameter) is far greater than the change in the constant which would enable cosmologists to decide between a closed, a flat or an open Universe.

Finally, knowing the exact relationship between the average density of the Universe and its critical density is also important for an accurate estimate of its age. As indicated earlier in this chapter, calculations based on the current rate at which galaxies are moving apart need to be adjusted to take account of the fact that they were moving apart more quickly when the Universe was younger. The size of the adjustment which needs to be made depends on what the average density of the Universe is believed to be. Although these uncertainties mean that cosmologists differ by a factor of two in their estimates of the age of the Universe, being able to work out what is probably the correct order of magnitude for the age of the Universe is itself a major scientific achievement.

Box 5I The critical density of the Universe and the Hubble constant

If a galaxy of mass m is at a distance r from the location of the big bang, its velocity v is given by:

$$v = H_0 r$$

where H_0 is the Hubble constant.

The kinetic energy of the galaxy is, therefore:

$$\tfrac{1}{2}m(H_0 r)^2$$

The net gravitational force acting on the galaxy is due to the mass of the Universe within a sphere of radius r.
This mass M is given by:

$$M = \tfrac{4}{3}\pi r^3 \rho$$

(where ρ is the density of the Universe), and the net gravitational force F acting on the galaxy is given by:

$$F = G\frac{Mm}{r^2}$$

The work which must be done by the galaxy to escape from the rest of the Universe is given by:

$$\int_r^\infty G\frac{Mm}{r^2}\,dr = \frac{GMm}{r}$$

i.e. (mass of galaxy) × (gravitational potential at r).

The critical density (ρ_c or Ω) of the Universe – at which the galaxy has just enough kinetic energy to escape – is given by:

$$\tfrac{1}{2}m(H_0 r)^2 = \frac{Gm}{r}\,(\tfrac{4}{3}\pi r^3 \rho_c)$$

That is,

$$\rho_c = \frac{3H_0^2}{8\pi G}$$

[Note. The calculation should, strictly speaking, be made using the general theory of relativity rather than Newton's gravitational theory.]

SAQ 5.15

Calculate ρ_c (or Ω) in the SI units $\mathrm{kg\,m^{-3}}$, where

$$\frac{1}{H_0} = 2\times10^{10}\text{ years and } G = 6.67\times10^{-11}\,\mathrm{N\,m^2\,kg^{-2}}.$$

SUMMARY

- Olbers showed that, according to Newton's cosmology – a uniform, infinite and static Universe – the sky at night could not be dark.

- The red-shift of identifiable lines in the spectra from galaxies can be explained in terms of the Doppler effect, i.e. $\frac{\Delta\lambda}{\lambda} = \frac{v}{c}$.

- The speed of recession of galaxies is directly proportional to their distance (Hubble's law) and implies that the Universe is expanding.

- Hubble's constant (H_0) is $\frac{\text{speed of recession}}{\text{distance}}$.

- The idea of an expanding Universe:
  - explains why the sky is dark at night;
  - suggests that the Universe began with a big bang;
  - enables cosmologists to estimate the age of the Universe (15–18 billion years).

- If units for H_0 are $\frac{\text{fraction of speed of light}}{\text{light-years}}$ then $\frac{1}{H_0}$ = age in years.

- The big bang theory of the Universe, i.e. that the Universe as we know it today developed by expansion and cooling from a very hot, very small beginning, is further supported by:
  - the existence of a 2.7K microwave background, which is the remnant of earlier, hotter radiation;
  - the large amount of helium in the Universe, most of which was produced when the Universe as a whole (rather than separate stars) provided the conditions needed for hydrogen burning to occur.

- According to modern cosmological theory, as the Universe cooled and expanded from the start of the big bang, matter became increasingly organised in the following sequence:
  - chaotic inter-conversion of photons and heavy particles of matter;
  - quarks and electrons;
  - protons, neutrons and electrons;
  - nuclei of helium;
  - atoms of hydrogen and helium;
  - clumping, resulting in stars – within galaxies – within clusters.

- Experimental evidence relating to temperatures of 10^{15}K, only a small fraction of a second after the start of the big bang, has been obtained from particle accelerators.

- Whether the Universe continues to expand without limit, approaches a limit or collapses to a big crunch depends on whether it is open, flat or closed. This in turn depends on whether the average density is smaller than, equal to or greater than the critical density.

- The critical density ρ_c (or Ω) is given by the expression $\frac{3H_0^2}{8\pi G}$.

- Though the average density and the critical density of the Universe are approximately equal, we cannot measure either accurately enough to be sure. This uncertainty also affects calculations of the age of the Universe.

Question

1 The intensity of stellar radiation at different wavelengths is often measured electronically.

Figure 5.8 shows the hydrogen emission line peaks from the visible spectrum of the radio source 3C 273.

a What is unusual about the spectral hydrogen lines of 3C 273?

b Calculate the recessional speed of 3C 273 and hence estimate its distance.

c What name is given to radio sources such as 3C 273?

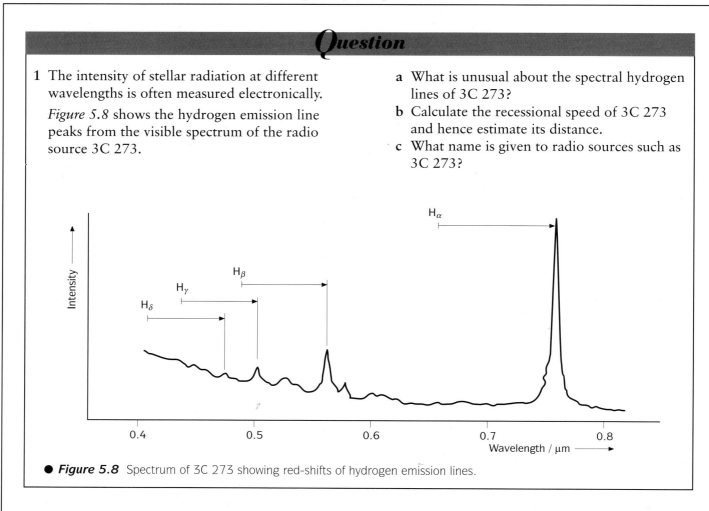

● *Figure 5.8* Spectrum of 3C 273 showing red-shifts of hydrogen emission lines.

Chapter six

The special theory of relativity

By the end of this chapter you should be able to:

1 understand the basic principles of the special theory of relativity;

2 show awareness of some of the predictions of the special theory of relativity;

3 quote observational evidence which matches the predictions and therefore supports the theory.

Although Albert Einstein *(figure 6.1)* was primarily a theoretical physicist, his theories of relativity have had an enormous influence on astronomy and cosmology during the twentieth century. Many examples of this influence have been included in chapters 1–5. In this chapter, Einstein's ideas about relativity are themselves the main focus of attention.

Einstein's **special theory of relativity**, published in 1905:

■ showed that the ideas of absolute space and absolute time, which had been key ideas in the strongly Newtonian physics and cosmology of the previous two centuries, were mistaken;

■ implied that matter and energy were inter-convertible, an idea which was important both for understanding the thermonuclear reactions which power stars and for developments in particle physics of ideas which enabled cosmologists to work out what probably happened during the big bang.

Einstein developed his special theory of relativity to resolve a problem about light and other forms of electromagnetic radiation. In 1865, James Clerk Maxwell had shown that light and other forms of radiation are wave-like disturbances in an electromagnetic field. According to Maxwell's theory, electromagnetic radiation of all types – i.e. of all wavelengths – always travels at exactly the same speed in empty space. All motion must, however, be measured relative to something that is regarded as being stationary. The following question therefore arose: relative to what fixed point, or **frame of reference**, do all electromagnetic waves always travel at the same speed? Since familiar waves such as water waves and sound waves travel through a substance, usually referred to as a **medium**, physicists proposed that electromagnetic radiation also travelled through an otherwise undetectable medium, called the **ether**, which pervaded the whole of space. The common speed of all types of electromagnetic radiation would then be its speed through the ether which was itself regarded as being stationary.

The idea of the ether was very similar to Newton's idea of absolute space: it was the framework within which the stars and galaxies were positioned and through which the planets moved. As the Earth moves in its orbit around the Sun, therefore, it must also travel through the ether and this suggested a way of testing the theory: there should be a difference in the speed of light depending on whether it is measured along the direction of the Earth's movement through the

● *Figure 6.1* Albert Einstein.

ether or at right angles to that direction. In 1887, this prediction was very carefully tested by Albert Michelson and Edward Morley whose apparatus was capable of detecting a difference in the speed of light ten times smaller than that to be expected from the speed of the Earth's movement through the ether *(box 6A)*. Michelson and Morley were unable, however, to detect any difference in the speed of light measured along and across the direction of the Earth's motion. Their experiment cast doubt, therefore, on the whole idea of an ether.

Einstein also rejected the idea of an ether and the related idea of absolute space, but did so on the basis of theory rather than experiment. To understand Einstein's reasoning, it is best to begin by considering Newton's ideas about motion.

Newton realised that all bodies have **inertia**, i.e. they tend to resist any change in their motion. This important idea is expressed in Newton's first law of motion: any body continues in its state of uniform motion, i.e. remains at rest or moves at a steady speed along a straight line, unless it is acted on by an external force.

On Earth, however, bodies which are thrown or dropped clearly do not continue in a state of uniform motion. They accelerate towards the Earth's centre and this acceleration is explained in terms of the external force of gravity which acts on them. But we can, like Newton, imagine situations in which bodies would obey his first law of motion. A spaceship in interstellar space, for example, far away from any significant gravitational influences, would provide a frame of reference relative to which a body would remain stationary or move with a steady velocity unless we deliberately exerted a force on it. A frame of reference in

Box 6A The Michelson–Morley experiment

The basic idea of the experiment is shown in *figure 6.2a*.

Light travelling along the direction of the Earth's motion through the ether would travel faster on its journey towards mirror X, but more slowly on its return.

Light travelling across the direction of the Earth's motion through the ether, would travel at the same speed before and after reflection from mirror Y. If, however, the Earth is moving through the ether with a velocity of v, this light would travel a distance of $d\sqrt{(1+v^2/c^2)}$ in each direction *(figure 6.2b)*.

Michelson and Morley observed the interference patterns with the apparatus in one orientation and then looked for any changes in the interference patterns as they rotated their apparatus through 90 degrees. This procedure meant that the distances to mirrors X and Y did not need to be exactly equal.

To avoid vibrations and distortions due to stopping and starting, the apparatus was kept slowly rotating, at 6 revolutions per minute, on a bath of mercury. They also repeated their observations three months later just in case the movement through the ether of the whole solar system itself was cancelling out the movement of the Earth through the ether as it orbited the Sun.

Though the apparatus was capable of measuring a shift in the interference pattern ten times smaller than that expected from the speed of the Earth around its orbit, no shift was observed.

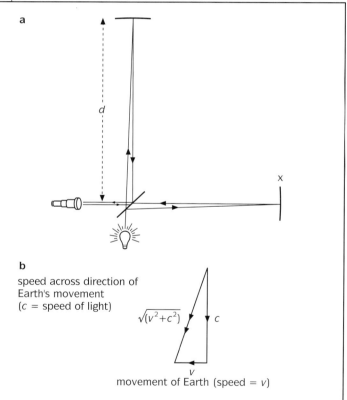

● *Figure 6.2* The Michelson–Morley experiment.

a Light from a single source is split into two perpendicular directions by a half-reflecting mirror. When beams rejoin at telescope, interference fringes are produced.

b Effective distance travelled across direction of Earth's movement is given by considering the addition of the velocity vectors.

which Newton's first law of motion is obeyed is known as an **inertial frame**.

It is important to realise that, although an inertial frame cannot have an acceleration, it may have a constant velocity. Any such constant velocity which a spaceship, for example, might have would be shared by everything inside the spaceship. No observations made inside the space-ship itself would enable an observer to detect this velocity. It is also important to note that, despite the acceleration produced by the Earth's gravity, it is legitimate in the thought-experiments described later in this chapter to regard a vehicle on the surface of the Earth as comprising an inertial frame so far as any *horizontal* forces and movements are concerned, provided that it has no horizontal acceleration. Again, there is no limit to the number of these restricted inertial frames, each of which is moving relative to each of the others.

Newton's idea of an inertial frame and Maxwell's discovery that all types of electro-magnetic radiation must always travel at the same speed through space were the two key ideas under-lying Einstein's special theory of relativity. It was by combining and extending these ideas that Einstein came up with his startling new theory.

Einstein took Newton's idea that the laws of motion apply in exactly the same way to any inertial frame and extended it to include *all* the laws of physics, not just the laws of motion. The idea that all the laws of physics apply equally to all inertial frames is sometimes called the **first postulate of special relativity**.

Einstein then extended this idea further by treating the common speed of all electromagnetic radiation, calculated by Maxwell, as being itself a fundamental law of physics which must, therefore, apply equally to all inertial frames of reference. In other words, from whatever inertial frame the speed of light – or of any other type of electromagnetic radiation – is measured, that speed will always be found to be exactly the same. This idea is sometimes called the **second postulate of special relativity**.

If electromagnetic radiation travels with exactly the same speed relative to any inertial frame, and there can be any number of inertial frames all moving relative to each other, the idea of an ether no longer makes any sense. In other words, accepting the special theory of relativity means abandoning the idea of the ether, together with the associated Newtonian idea of an absolute space existing independently of particular bodies such as planets, stars and galaxies.

Furthermore, by combining the ideas:

- first, that the speed of light is the same when measured from any inertial frame;
- second, that there is a constant relative velocity between any pair of inertial frames;

Einstein's special theory of relativity generated some very surprising predictions.

The basic principle underlying these predictions is very simple. Since

$$\text{speed} = \frac{\text{distance}}{\text{time}}$$

and the speed of light is the *same* when measured by observers who are moving relative to each other, the measurements of time and distance which are made by these observers must be *different*. Furthermore, it makes no sense to ask which particular measurements of time and distance are correct. All such measurements are made from within some inertial frame and there is no reason to give any particular frame of reference an especially privileged status.

Time dilation

One of the predictions of the special theory of rela-tivity is that two observers who are moving relative to each other will each think that the other's clock is running slow. This can be demonstrated, as can many of the implications of relativity, by a tactic often used by Einstein – and by Newton before him – namely a **thought-experiment**.

Imagine two observers travelling in opposite directions on parallel railway tracks. The coaches on which the observers are travelling each carry a long plane mirror facing the other coach (*figure 6.3a*). If either observer sends a pulse of light, at right angles to the direction they are travelling, this pulse would then be reflected between the two mirrors over and over again. Each observer could use these reflections as the basis for a clock: one tick of the clock is the time taken for light to travel from an observer's own mirror to the other observer's mirror and back again.

From the point of view of either observer, however, the pulse of light originally sent by the other observer travels a greater distance between reflections than the pulse of light originally sent by themselves *(figure 6.3b,c)*. Since travelling a greater distance at the same speed takes a longer time, both observers find that the other observer's clock is ticking more slowly than their own clock. To put the same point in a different way, the time interval between two events which occur in a particular inertial frame is longer when measured by an observer who is moving relative to that inertial frame than it is when measured by an observer who is within the same inertial frame.

This relativistic slowing of a moving clock compared to a stationary one is known as **time dilation**. The effect applies to any type of clock, including the metabolic processes and ageing of our own bodies. It is also important to recognise that, in the absence of any specially favoured or absolute frame of reference, it makes no sense to ask which of two clocks in relative motion is going at the right speed or which of two observers in relative motion correctly measures the time interval between two events.

Experimental evidence for time dilation has been provided by

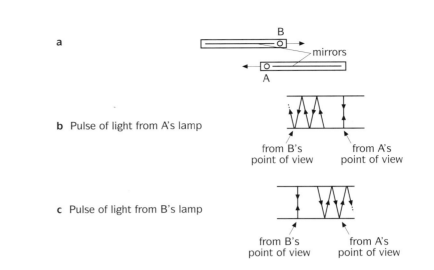

● **Figure 6.3** Time dilation thought-experiment.
[Note. Strictly, there would need to be a *set* of synchronised light-pulse clocks in each vehicle, located where the successive reflections of the other person's pulse of light arrive. These reflected pulses would get progressively out of step with the synchronised clocks.]

particles called muons which can be created by collisions in particle accelerators. The extremely short lifetime of these particles, as measured by the scientists using the particle accelerator, can be greatly increased by accelerating the particles to 99.7% of the speed of light. Muons are also created when cosmic radiation strikes the Earth's upper atmosphere. The relatively high proportion of these muons which survive long enough to reach the Earth's surface can also be explained in terms of time dilation *(box 6B)*.

SAQ 6.1

From the point of view of an observer on Earth, a clock on a fast-moving spaceship runs slow. A scientist on the spaceship, however, finds that bacteria still divide at the same rate as they did when the spaceship was on the launch-pad.

How can the observer on Earth explain this?

Length contraction

The special theory of relativity predicts that two observers who are moving relative to each other will disagree not only about their measurements of time but also about their measurements of distance. Once again, this idea can be demonstrated by a thought-experiment.

The length of a train can be compared with the length of a tunnel by arranging switches to make lamps come on: lamp X, at one end

Box 6B Muons and cosmic radiation

When cosmic radiation strikes the upper layers of the Earth's atmosphere, muons are created. Since these have a half-life of only 2 microseconds (2×10^{-6}s) only a very small proportion would be expected to reach the Earth's surface, in the absence of time dilation, even though they travel at more than 99% of the speed of light.

The half-life of muons, however, is a type of clock and, like other clocks, appears to run slow when moving relative to an observer. In fact, the apparent half-life of the fast-moving muons is increased to about 20 microseconds.

Muons take about 20 microseconds to travel from a height of 6 km to sea-level. This is 10 normal half-lives so that the number of muons recorded at sea-level should be 2^{10} less than at 6 km, i.e. only about 0.1%. However, because time dilation increases the half-life of the muons, as measured by an observer who is at rest relative to the muons, to 20 microseconds, the number of muons recorded at sea-level is about 50% of the number recorded at 6 km.

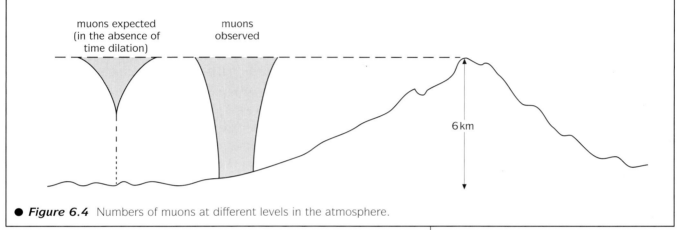

● **Figure 6.4** Numbers of muons at different levels in the atmosphere.

of the tunnel, comes on when the front of the train emerges and lamp Y, at the other end of the tunnel, comes on when the rear of the train enters (*figure 6.5*). Suppose observer A, by the track at a point mid-way through the tunnel, sees the lights come on simultaneously. For this observer, the train will be exactly the same length as the tunnel. For observer B, however, who is on the train at its mid-point and is travelling towards lamp X and away from

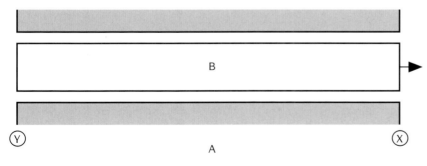

● **Figure 6.5** Length contraction thought-experiment.
Observer A sees lamps X and Y light simultaneously, indicating that the train and the tunnel are exactly the same length.
As the light is travelling from the lamps, observer B moves towards lamp X and away from lamp Y and so sees lamp X light before lamp Y. This indicates that the front of the train has exited the tunnel before the rear of the train has entered, i.e. that the train is longer than the tunnel.

lamp Y, lamp X will come on before lamp Y. For observer B, therefore, the front of the train emerges from the tunnel before the rear of the train enters the tunnel. Observer B concludes, therefore, that the train is longer than the tunnel.

In other words, the length of an object as measured by an observer relative to whom the object is moving is smaller than the length of that object as measured by an observer from within the same inertial frame as the object. This effect is known as **length contraction.**

As with time dilation, length contraction is completely symmetrical. If the lights are attached to the ends of the train rather than to the ends of the tunnel, they will then come on simultaneously for observer B, who concludes that the train and the tunnel are the same length. Lamp Y, however, is moving towards observer A, and lamp X is moving away. Observer A, therefore, sees lamp Y come on before lamp X. This indicates that the rear of the train has entered the tunnel before the front has moved out of the tunnel, so observer A concludes that the tunnel is longer than the train. As before, it is the observer who is moving relative to the object being measured who judges its length to be smaller than an observer in the same inertial frame as the object.

Once again, as with time dilation, it makes no sense to ask which of the observers makes the correct comparison: all comparisons of length are made from within some inertial frame and there is no reason to favour any particular frame. The idea of the proper length of an object – i.e. of its length as measured by an observer who is at rest with respect to the object – is, however, a useful one. It should also be noted that length contraction occurs only along the direction of the relative motion.

SAQ 6.2

From the point of view of an observer on Earth, an object in a fast-moving spaceship becomes shorter. An astronaut in the spaceship, however, finds that the length of the object, as measured with a ruler, is exactly the same as when the spaceship was on the launch-pad.

How can the observer on Earth explain this?

Special relativity, mass and energy

When the theory of special relativity is applied to the concepts of momentum and kinetic energy, it predicts that the observed mass of a body should increase as its velocity relative to an observer increases.

At everyday speeds, which are small compared to the speed of light, the increase in a body's mass due to its relative velocity is exceedingly small.

The greater the relative velocity of a body, however, the greater the observed mass. Furthermore, as the relative velocity of a body approaches the speed of light, its observed mass becomes very large indeed *(box 6C)*.

These predictions of the special theory of relativity have the following very important implications:

1 Because everyday speeds are small compared to the speed of light, the mass of a body can be regarded as constant. Newton's second law of motion relating force and acceleration can, therefore, still be applied.

2 Because the mass of a body increases with its relative velocity, the greater its relative velocity already is, the more difficult it becomes to accelerate it further.

Box 6C Why we don't normally notice relativistic time dilation, length contraction and mass increase

The factor by which time dilates, length contracts and mass increases as a result of relative motion is

where *v* is the velocity of the object being observed relative to the observer, and *c* is the velocity of light.

As *table 6.1* indicates, the extent of the relativistic changes in observed time, length or mass is extremely small unless the relative velocity is a significant percentage of the velocity of light.

Relative velocity/ % *velocity of light*	*Observed length* (rest length 100 m)	*Observed time* (rest time 1 hour)/ h : min : s	*Observed mass* (rest mass 1 kg, i.e. 1000 g)
1%	99.99 m	1:00:02	1000.1 g
10%	99.5 m	1:00:18	1005 g
50%	86.6 m	1:09	1155 g
90%	43.6 m	2:18	2294 g
99%	14.1 m	7:05	7092 g

● *Table 6.1* Extent of relativistic changes

3 Because the mass of a body tends towards infinity as its relative velocity approaches the speed of light, it is impossible for that velocity ever to reach the speed of light.

According to the special theory of relativity, therefore, the speed of light is not only the same from all frames of reference, it is also a limiting speed which can be approached but never actually attained by bodies having mass.

Plenty of experimental evidence supporting the above predictions about the relationship between rest mass and relativistic mass has been obtained using particle accelerators.

According to the special theory of relativity, the work done on a body increases the kinetic energy of that body, not only by increasing the speed of the body but also by increasing its mass. This strongly suggests that mass and energy are not entirely independent of each other. In fact, the special theory of relativity requires that mass and energy are inter-convertible at a 'rate of exchange' given by the expression:

$$E = \Delta m c^2$$

Once again, Einstein took two existing scientific ideas – in this case the ideas that in collisions, chemical reactions, etc., mass and energy are each conserved – and combined them into a single idea with important implications. The idea that mass and energy are inter-convertible, and that it is the total mass-plus-energy which is conserved, played an important part in cosmologists' understanding both of the thermonuclear reactions which power stars and of many of the processes which occurred at the early stages of the big bang.

Box 6D Einstein's general theory of relativity

In 1915, Einstein published his general theory of relativity. This is essentially a theory of gravity, the force which dominates the Universe on a large scale.

According to the general theory of relativity, what scientists since Newton have regarded as a gravitational field is a distortion of space itself in the region of a massive body. This alternative account of gravity not only explains everything which Newton's theory explains, but also observations which cannot be accounted for on Newton's theory, for example the observed changes in the orbit of the planet Mercury *(figure 6.6)*.

Mercury's elliptical orbit slowly rotates (precesses). The observed rate of this rotation cannot be explained by Newton's theory of gravity but exactly matches the value calculated from the general theory of relativity.

The general theory of relativity also predicts that light should be deflected when it passes close to a massive body. This prediction was confirmed, in 1919, by measuring the deflection of light from a star by the Sun's gravitational field during a solar eclipse. More recently, observations of the deflection by the Sun of the radiation from powerful radio sources known as quasars have also confirmed the theory.

Soon after Einstein published his general theory of relativity, Karl Schwarzschild realised that a very large and very concentrated mass – which might, for example, occur as matter collapses in the core of a very massive star – would make space so tightly curved that not even radiation could escape from it. The idea of a black hole had been born.

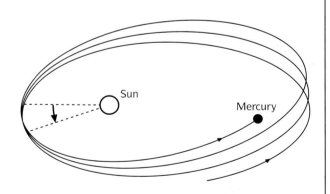

● *Figure 6.6* Precession of Mercury's perihelion.
The perihelion of Mercury's orbit rotates (precesses) at 574 arc-seconds per century.
Calculations using Newton's theory of gravity show that:

Venus causes	277 arc-seconds
Earth causes	90 arc-seconds
Jupiter causes	153 arc-seconds
others cause	11 arc-seconds
TOTAL	531 arc-seconds

SUMMARY

- The special theory of relativity postulates that:
  - the laws of physics are the same in all inertial (i.e. unaccelerated) frames of reference;
  - the speed of light for any observer in any inertial frame is always the same.

- The theory of special relativity implies that there is no stationary medium (ether) through which electromagnetic radiation travels and no absolute space independent of matter. This view is supported by the Michelson–Morley experiment.

- The theory implies that:
  - a clock which is moving relative to an observer will appear to run slow – this time dilation can be demonstrated with muons whose half-life appears to a stationary observer to increase when they are accelerated to high speeds;
  - an object which is moving relative to an observer will appear to be shorter, in the direction of its travel, than it does to an observer who is at rest with respect to (i.e. in the same inertial frame as) the object – this effect is known as length contraction;
  - the observed mass of an object when it is moving relative to the observer is greater than its rest mass.

- In each case the size of the relativistic change is extremely small unless the relative velocity between the observer and the object being observed is a significant percentage of the velocity of light.

- The theory also implies that mass and energy are inter-convertible in accordance with the equation $E = \Delta mc^2$.

Question

1 According to Newton's theory of 1686, the acceleration produced in a body of mass m by a force F is given by

$$a = \frac{F}{m}$$

According to Einstein's special theory of relativity (1905), the acceleration produced is given by

$$a = \frac{F}{m} \sqrt{\left(1 - \frac{v^2}{c^2}\right)^3}$$

How do the accelerations predicted by Newton and Einstein compare:

a at the speeds of ordinary bodies on Earth (e.g. balls, vehicles etc.)?

b at speeds approaching the speed of light?

Explain your answers.

Answers to self-assessment questions

Prelude

P.1 $(3.00 \times 10^8) \times (3.15 \times 10^7) = 9.45 \times 10^{15}$ m

The figure 10^{16} m is, therefore, correct to within about 5%.

P.2 **a** One-sixth of a circle = one-sixth of a day, i.e. 4 hours. [Note. This is only approximately correct because the Sun's azimuth does not, in general, change uniformly with time.]

b See *figure*. The difference in the directions of the rising and the setting Sun is 180°. The noon shadow is shorter than at midwinter because the Sun is higher in the sky.

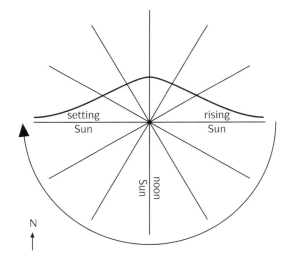

● *Answer for* SAQ P.2b.

P.3 **a** 180°

b 180° divided by 182.6 days (i.e. half of the 365.25 days in a year) gives just under 1°.

P.4 **a** See *figure*.

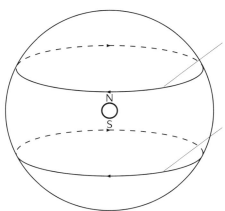

daily path of the Sun when at X on ecliptic (always visible from Earth's north pole)

daily path of the Sun when at Y on ecliptic (never visible from Earth's north pole)

● *Answer for* SAQ P.4a.

b The Sun never rises.

P.5 See *figure*.

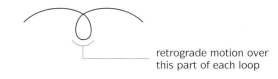

retrograde motion over this part of each loop

● *Answer for* SAQ P.5.

Chapter 1

1.1 Mars is in retrograde motion when it is on the opposite side of the Earth from the Sun (in opposition) and hence closest to Earth. The closer Mars is, the brighter it looks.

1.2 The angular separation changes from 50° to 10°, i.e. the parallax is 40°.

1.3 The angular separation changes from 3.5° to 2.5°, i.e. the parallax is 1°.

1.4 The graph would be a straight line through the origin. (T^2 and d^3 are directly proportional.)

1.5 $T^2 = 1.52^3$ gives $T = \sqrt{3.51}$. So the orbital period of Mars is 1.87 years.

1.6 $d^3 = (12)^2$ gives $d = \sqrt[3]{144}$. So Jupiter is approximately 5.24 AU from the Sun.

1.7 The mean distance of Saturn from the Sun is:

  a $9.54 \times 1.5 \times 10^{11} = 1.43 \times 10^{12}$ m;

  b $\dfrac{1.43 \times 10^{12}}{3 \times 10^8} = 4.77 \times 10^3$ light-seconds (79.5 light-minutes).

1.8 **a** Venus appears as a crescent when it is between the Earth and the Sun (in inferior conjunction) and appears full when it is on the opposite side of the Sun from Earth (in superior conjunction). Venus looks bigger when closer.

  b Venus is always on the same side of the Earth as the Sun and is, therefore, only seen around dusk and dawn.

1.9 Their periods can be observed and the relative sizes of their orbits estimated by comparing their maximum separation from Jupiter. [Note. This assumes that they all move in the same plane.]

1.10 [Note. SI units must be used in this calculation.]

$$m_s = \frac{4\pi^2 d^3}{GT^2}$$

$$= \frac{4(3.142)^2 \times (1.5 \times 10^{11})^3}{6.67 \times 10^{-11} \times (3.15 \times 10^7)^2}$$

$$= 2 \times 10^{30}\,\text{kg}$$

1.11 Pluto is much less massive than other planets, has a more eccentric orbit (which cuts inside Neptune's orbit at one point) and is at a bigger angle to the plane of the Earth's orbit around the Sun (the ecliptic).

End-of-chapter questions

1 **a** See figure.

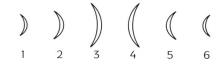

b The prediction from the Ptolemaic model does not match the observed phases of Venus (see *figure 1.5*), whereas the prediction made from the Copernican model does. Copernicus himself was aware that Venus was a crucial test between his system and the Ptolemaic system but, since the telescope had not been invented, could not actually make the necessary observations.

2 **a**

0	3	6	12	24	48	96
4	7	10	16	28	52	100
0.4	0.7	1.0	1.6	2.8	5.2	10.0

b The 1st, 2nd, 3rd, 4th, 6th and 7th figures match the distances (in AU) of Mercury, Venus, Earth, Mars, Jupiter and Saturn.

c (i) Astronomers predicted that other planets would be found corresponding to 5th figure in the series (i.e. 2.8 AU) and also for the 8th figure (19.6 AU) and beyond.

(ii) The predictions led to the discovery of Uranus in 1781 and of Ceres – one of many asteroids – in 1801, both very close to the predicted positions. Though the planets Neptune and Pluto were subsequently discovered, their distances do not fit the Bode–Titus series of numbers.

Though the Bode–Titus series of numbers may be purely accidental, it might relate to the long-term stability of the orbits of planets which perturb each other.

Chapter 2

2.1 Brightness is proportional to $\dfrac{1}{d^2}$, so Sirius is $\sqrt{10^{12}} = 10^6$ times further away than the Sun. This suggests that the distance of Sirius from Earth is about $\dfrac{1.5 \times 10^{11} \times 10^6}{10^{16}} = 15$ light-years.

(The currently accepted figure is 8.7 light-years.)

2.2 A parallax of 0.76 arc-seconds implies that the star is $\dfrac{1}{0.76} = 1.32$ pc (4.29 light-years) distant.

2.3 100 pc = 326 light-years.

2.4 a The difference in magnitude is 3, so the intensity ratio equals 2.5^3, i.e. 15.6.

b The difference in magnitudes of the Sun and Sirius is about 25. A difference in magnitude of 5 means an intensity ratio of 100. So a difference in magnitude of 25 means an intensity ratio of $(100)^5$, i.e. 10^{10}.

2.5 The absolute magnitude of Arcturus is:

$$M = -0.1 - 5\log(\tfrac{11}{10})$$

$$= -0.1 - 5(0.04)$$

$$= -0.3$$

2.6 The period is about 5.75 days. The magnitude decreases (i.e. brightness rises) at about twice the rate it decreases (i.e. brightness falls). The magnitude changes by 0.7, i.e. an intensity ratio of $2.5^{0.7} = 1.9$.

2.7 A period of 4 days implies Polaris has an absolute magnitude of -3.1.

$$-3.1 = 2 - 5\log\frac{d}{10}$$

That is,

$$\log\frac{d}{10} = 1.02$$

$$d = 10(10)^{1.02} = 104.7\,\text{pc}$$

The distance of Polaris from Earth is about 104.7 parsec, i.e. 341 light-years.

2.8 Using SI units throughout, the mass m_G of the galaxy is about:

$$m_G = \frac{4\pi^2 d^3}{GT^2}$$

$$= \frac{4(3.142)^2 \times (3 \times 10^4 \times 10^{16})^3}{6.67 \times 10^{-11} \times (2.3 \times 10^8 \times 3.15 \times 10^7)^2}$$

$$= 3 \times 10^{41}\,\text{kg}$$

The total mass of the galaxy will be greater than this, though not in proportion to the area of the galactic disc outside the Sun's orbit since there is evidence of a large concentration of mass at the centre.

Note also the recent evidence that each part of the outer disc of a galaxy often has the same rotational velocity irrespective of its distance from the galactic centre. This suggests that there is a huge unseen halo of dark matter.

2.9 a Using $M - m = -5\log\left(\dfrac{d}{10}\right)$:

$$-29 = -5\log\frac{d}{10}$$

So

$$d = 10(10)^{5.8}$$

The galaxy is at a distance of $6.3 \times 10^6\,\text{pc}$ (2×10^6 light-years).

b This distance is about 20 times the diameter of the Milky Way.

2.10

Method used	Distances measured
Parallax	up to about 300 light-years (including some Cepheid variables)
Cepheids	up to 2.5 million light-years (including some galaxies)
Brightness	5 billion light-years (assuming equal brightness of galaxies)

[Note. Red-shifts are often used to estimate distances beyond this, on the assumption that Hubble's law holds true. See chapter 5.]

2.11 The maximum difference in magnitude from the average is 1.25. This represents a brightness ratio of $2.5^{1.25} = 3.14$ and hence a distance ratio of $\sqrt{3.14}$, i.e. 1.77.

Hubble's estimates of galactic distances could be wrong by this factor.

End-of-chapter question

1 The galaxy is rotating in the plane of the line of sight.

Since the speed of movement of stars in the bulge is directly proportional to their distance from the centre of the galaxy, the stars in this area must be rotating with the same *angular* speed.

The more widely separated stars in the disc of the galaxy are all moving with the same speed. Since their speed is not what Kepler's laws would lead us to expect (i.e. varying inversely with their distance from the centre of the galaxy), astronomers believe that there must be a very consideable amount of unseen (dark) matter surrounding the visible outer edge of the galaxy.

Chapter 3

3.1 Ordering the stars by temperature, starting with the hottest, gives: Rigel, Sirius, Arcturus, Betelgeuse.

3.2 From *figure 3.3*, λ_{max} is 0.48×10^{-6} m. Now:

$\lambda_{max} \times T = 2.9 \times 10^{-3}$

So

$$T = \frac{2.9 \times 10^{-3}}{0.48 \times 10^{-6}}$$

$$= 6.0 \times 10^{3} \, \text{K}$$

The temperature of the Sun's surface is about 6000 K.

3.3 The Sun is a main sequence star of average size.

3.4 In the vapour state, atoms do not interact with each other. They emit specific wavelengths of light related to the particular energy levels between which electrons in the atoms jump. These energy levels are different in different types of atom.

3.5 The element iron is present in the Sun's atmosphere.

End-of-chapter question

1 Because the motion of the stars is related they are probably a binary pair orbiting their common centre of mass; as one of the stars is moving away from Earth the other moves towards Earth.

The orbital period for the binary pair is about 27 days.

The pair of stars as a whole is moving away from Earth with a velocity of about $10 \, \text{km s}^{-1}$.

Chapter 4

4.1 The amount of energy which would be released by a loss in mass of 1 g is:

$E = (0.001) (3 \times 10^{8})^{2} = 9 \times 10^{13} \, \text{J}$

4.2 The Sun's annual rate of loss of mass is:

$$\frac{(4 \times 10^{26}) \times (3.15 \times 10^{7})}{(3 \times 10^{8})^{2}}$$

$$= 1.4 \times 10^{17} \, \text{kg year}^{-1}$$

The time it will take to lose 0.035% of its present mass is:

$$\frac{\text{mass consumed}}{\text{rate}}$$

$$= \frac{(0.035 \times 10^{-2}) \times (2 \times 10^{30})}{1.4 \times 10^{17}}$$

$$= 5 \times 10^{9} \, \text{years}$$

i.e. 5 billion years.

4.3 A star's lifetime on the main sequence decreases by a very large proportion for a relatively small increase in mass. The greater the mass of the star, the greater the temperature needed to produce enough radiation pressure to maintain equilibrium and the greater the equilibrium pressure. Both these factors will increase the rate of hydrogen burning.

Even when a log–log graph is plotted from *table 4.1*, a straight line is not obtained, so there is no simple relationship between a star's lifetime on the main sequence and its mass.

4.4 The temperature of the core will not become high enough to ignite hydrogen burning. The body will gradually cool once gravitational collapse is complete. The planets may well have been formed in this way.

4.5 As they are forming, main sequence stars will be cooler but also larger than when they reach the main sequence. They will, therefore, be towards the right-hand side of the H–R diagram. Whether they are above or below the main sequence line depends on whether the coolness or the size has the greater effect on the rate at which radiation is emitted.

4.6 This suggests that Cepheid variables may be main sequence stars in the process of developing into red giants.

4.7 The commonest elements in the Sun are hydrogen and helium from the gas clouds out of which the Sun formed. Hydrogen burning in the Sun's core will have converted hydrogen to helium but cannot have created the other elements. These must all have been created in an earlier star, for example a red giant, material from which became caught up in the gas cloud from which the Sun was formed. The Sun cannot, therefore, be a first-generation star, i.e. formed exclusively from primordial hydrogen and helium.

4.8 Elements with more massive nuclei than iron are produced only in supernova explosions. The gas cloud from which the Sun was formed must, therefore, have included the debris from such an explosion.

4.9 Stars spend a greater proportion of their time as main sequence stars than as red giants or as white dwarfs emitting enough radiation to be seen. Furthermore, not all red giants become white dwarfs.

4.10 Only those pulsars whose narrow beam of radiation is sometimes directed towards Earth will be detected.

4.11 The pulses can be detected electronically. Alternatively, the star can be viewed strobo-scopically, i.e. intermittently at the same rate as it is flashing, when it is possible to make it 'disappear'.

End-of-chapter questions

1   Star A changes from a main sequence star of medium magnitude and temperature to a red giant and then to a white dwarf.

Star B changes from a brighter than average and hotter than average main sequence star to a red giant and then to a very bright supernova.

Star A is less massive than star B; the mass of star B, but not that of star A, exceeds the Chandrasekhar limit.

2   **a** Cluster Y is the youngest and cluster X the oldest.

The brightest and most massive stars also have the shortest lives so the youngest cluster has stars further along the main sequence and also has stars moving off into the red giant area from higher up the main sequence.

b Since Population I stars are younger they are more likely to include debris from older stars which have produced heavier metal elements via a series of thermonuclear reactions plus a supernova explosion. Older Population II stars are likely to comprise primarily primordial hydrogen and helium.

[Note. Population II stars are brighter than Population I stars. The difference is important when using Cepheid variables for distance estimates.]

Chapter 5

5.1 If the Universe were finite, there would be a gravitational force causing it to collapse towards its centre. In an infinite Universe, however, gravitational forces might act on any body equally in all directions and there would be no net force.

5.2 The red-shifts for galaxies B, C and D are 7 mm, 11 mm and 17 mm respectively, corresponding to recessional velocities of 4.7%, 7.3% and 11.3% of the speed of light.

5.3 Sirius and Earth are moving apart at $3 \times 10^8 \times 10^{-4} = 3 \times 10^4 \, \text{m s}^{-1}$.

5.4 A blue-shift indicates that the Andromeda galaxy is moving towards us.

Two local galaxies in the same local cluster could be moving towards each other. Alternatively the blue-shift could be due to the movement of the solar system around the centre of our own galaxy so that it is just our region of the Milky Way galaxy, not the galaxy as a whole, which is moving towards the Andromeda galaxy.

5.5   The age of the Universe can be calculated from any point on a Hubble graph because the Hubble constant is the constant of proportionality between the speed of recession of a galaxy and its distance.

5.6   The sky is dark at night because:
- fewer photons reach the Earth in a given time;
- the photons of red-shifted radiation are less energetic.

The idea that the Universe has a finite age suggests a further way of resolving Olbers' paradox. The night sky is dark because we receive light on Earth only from the finite part of the Universe within a distance of 15–18 billion light-years. Light from further away than this has not yet had time to get here. Some cosmologists believe that the Universe extends beyond this limit because there was an early **inflationary** period of the Universe when there was a faster-than-light expansion of space–time itself which would not violate the principle that nothing can travel faster than light.

5.7   To convert $\mathrm{km\,s^{-1}}$ to a fraction of the speed of light, multiply by $\dfrac{1}{3 \times 10^5}$; to change Mpc to light-years, multiply by 3.26×10^6.

So

$H_0 = 80\,\mathrm{km\,s^{-1}\,Mpc^{-1}}$

$= \dfrac{80}{(3 \times 10^5) \times (3.26 \times 10^6)}$

$= 8.2 \times 10^{-11}\,\mathrm{year^{-1}}$

The reciprocal of Hubble's constant $\dfrac{1}{H_0}$ gives an estimate of 12.2×10^9 years (12.2 billion years) for the age of the Universe. [But note the uncertainty, not only in the value of H_0, but also in how this varies with distance.]

5.8   Rearranging $\lambda_{\mathrm{max}} \times T = 2.9 \times 10^{-3}$ gives:

$\lambda_{\mathrm{max}} = \dfrac{2.9 \times 10^{-3}}{2.7}$

$= 1.07 \times 10^{-3}\,\mathrm{m}$

5.9   The fact that cosmic microwave radiation has the same intensity in all directions (apart from the very slight ripples referred to in the text and any Doppler shift due to the Earth's motion through it) indicates that the Universe is the same in all directions, i.e. isotropic. This is one aspect of its being everywhere the same.

5.10 There are several possible times for the end of the big bang:

0.001 second	protons and neutrons, the building bricks of ordinary matter, exist;
100 seconds	hydrogen and helium nuclei, from which stars are formed, exist;
10^4 seconds	hydrogen and helium atoms exist and the Universe is transparent to radiation.

5.11 The energies of collisions in particle accelerators are equivalent to temperatures of $10^{15}\,\mathrm{K}$, so there is some experimental evidence for what could have happened in the big bang back to about 10^{-12} seconds from its start.

5.12 Electrons and positrons have only about $\frac{1}{2000}$ of the mass of protons/anti-protons so that correspondingly less energy is needed to create them.

5.13 The wavelength of the cosmic background radiation has become enormously longer and its energy/mass value correspondingly smaller.

Except for relatively small mass → energy conversions in thermonuclear reactions, the total amount of matter in the Universe has remained more or less the same.

5.14 The big crunch could be followed by another big bang and the whole process repeated indefinitely.

5.15 The value of ρ_c (or Ω) in the SI units $kg\,m^{-3}$ is:

$$\frac{3}{(2 \times 10^{10} \times 3.15 \times 10^7)^2 \times 8 \times 3.142 \times 6.67 \times 10^{-11}}$$

$$= 4.5 \times 10^{-27}\,kg\,m^{-3}$$

(The mass of a proton is 1.7×10^{-27} kg, so this is just under 3 protons per cubic metre.)

End-of-chapter question

1   a The spectral lines are unusual in that they are *emission* lines rather than absorption lines and that they show an extremely large red-shift ($\frac{\Delta\lambda}{\lambda}$ of 14–15%). This is proportionally the same for any of the lines.

b From *figure 5.3*, a recessional speed of 14–15% of the speed of light implies a distance of about 3×10^9 light-years.

Alternatively, from *box 5D*, the Hubble constant H_0 is 5×10^{-11} year^{-1}.

Distance (light years)

$$= \frac{\text{speed of recession (fraction of speed of light)}}{\text{Hubble constant}}$$

$$= \frac{0.15}{5 \times 10^{-11}}$$

$$= 3 \times 10^9 \text{ light-years}$$

c 3C 273 is known as a quasi-stellar radio source or quasar.

Chapter 6

6.1   The rate of division of the bacteria – a biological clock – is slowed by exactly the same proportion, from the point of view of the external observer, as the clock which is used to time it.

6.2   From the point of view of the external observer, the length of the ruler has contracted by exactly the same proportion as the length of the object it is being used to measure.

End-of-chapter question

1   a If v is very much less than c, then $(1 - v^2/c^2)^{3/2}$ is very close to 1 so Einstein's formula gives the same answer as Newton's.

b As v approaches c, then $(1 - v^2/c^2)^{3/2}$ tends to 0 so the acceleration produced by a given force becomes smaller and smaller. When $v = c$, the acceleration produced is zero.

Index (Numbers in italics refer to figures.)